Controversial Issues in Environmental Policy

CONTROVERSIAL ISSUES IN PUBLIC POLICY

Series Editors
Dennis Palumbo and Rita Mae Kelly
Arizona State University

Controversial Issues in Environmental Policy

Science vs. Economics vs. Politics

Kent E. Portney

Controversial Issues in Public Policy
Volume 1

SAGE Publications
International Educational and Professional Publisher
Newbury Park   London   New Delhi

To Alexandra

For information address:

SAGE Publications, Inc.
2455 Teller Road
Newbury Park, California 91320

SAGE Publications Ltd.
6 Bonhill Street
London EC2A 4PU
United Kingdom

SAGE Publications India Pvt. Ltd.
M-32 Market
Greater Kailash I
New Delhi 110 048 India

Printed in the United States of America

Library of Congress Cataloging-in-Publication Data

Portney, Kent E.
   Controversial issues in environmental policy: science vs.
economics vs. politics / Kent E. Portney
      p.   cm.—(Controversial issues in public policy; v. 1)
   Includes bibliographical references and index.
   ISBN 0-8039-4221-4 (cloth).—ISBN 0-8039-4222-2 (pbk.)
   1. Environmental policy—United States.   2. Environmental
protection—United States.   3. Pollution—Economic aspects—United
States.   I. Title.   II. Series.
HC110.E5P66   1992   92-30004
333.7′0973—dc20   CIP

93 94 95   10 9 8 7 6 5 4 3 2

Sage Production Editor: Judith L. Hunter

Contents

Series Editors' Introduction

Public policy controversies escalated during the 1980s and early 1990s. This was partly due to bitter partisan debate between Republicans and Democrats, a divided government in which the Republicans controlled the Presidency and the Democrats controlled the Congress, and the rise of negative campaigning in the 1988 presidential election. In addition, the past decade was a time when highly controversial issues such as abortion, crime, environmental pollution, affirmative action, and choice in education became prominent in the public policy agenda.

Policy issues in this atmosphere tend to be framed in dichotomous, either-or terms. Abortion is depicted as "murder" on the one hand, or a woman's "self-interested choice" on the other. One is either "tough" on crime, or too much in favor of "defendants' rights." Affirmative action is a matter of "quotas" or a "special interest" issue. School choice is the means for correcting the "educational mess," or the destruction of public education. In such an atmosphere there doesn't seem to be a middle ground or a common ground where cooler heads can unite.

The shrillness of these policy disputes reduces the emphasis on finding rational, balanced solutions. Political ideology and a zero-sum approach to politics and policy became the order of the day.

Certainly, there hasn't been an end to ideology over the past decade and a half, as some believed was occurring in the 1970s. Reaganomics contributed to a widening gap between the rich and the poor during the 1980s, which exacerbated partisan debate and further stymied governmental action. In 1992 controversies over health care—both lack of coverage for millions and skyrocketing costs—illustrate the wide gap in the way Republicans and Democrats approach public policy controversies. The Reagan "revolution" was based on a definite and clear ideological approach to public policy in general: eliminate government regulation; reduce taxes; provide tax incentives for business; cut welfare; and privatize the delivery of governmental services. Democrats, of course, did not agree.

This series, Controversial Issues in Public Policy, is meant to shed more light and less ideological heat on major policy issues in substantive policy areas. In this volume, Kent Portney discusses such issues as acid rain, ozone depletion, air and water quality, and hazardous waste. As might be expected, none of these has an easy solution. In 1992, for example, President Bush, alarmed by new reports of more rapid ozone depletion than had previously been estimated, announced a speedup in the phaseout of ozone-destroying chemicals by American manufacturers. He was criticized for delaying so long before he acted and also for not doing enough in his new phaseout policy. But to successfully deal with ozone depletion, as Portney notes, requires action by all industrialized nations. The United States, Japan, and Germany were not terribly enthusiastic about taking action by themselves because it might make them less competitive in the world marketplace.

Portney describes how controversial issues in environmental policy get onto the policy agenda, how policies about the issues are formulated, and the difficulty in implementing such policies. Thus, his coverage goes beyond simply describing the nature of controversial environmental policy issues; he also demonstrates how the policy-making process tries to deal with the issues, for the policy-making process itself often detracts from finding solutions to the vital environmental issues facing the United States as we prepare to enter the twenty-first century.

RITA MAE KELLY
DENNIS PALUMBO

1

The Context of Environmental Policy-Making in America

This book is principally about public environmental policies in the United States, and many of the controversies surrounding these environmental policies. When people speak of controversies, they are usually speaking of disagreements between or among people. These disagreements sometimes focus on whether some event or trend can actually be considered an environmental problem worthy of public policy attention. For example, there will be a review of the debate about whether depletion of the ozone layer of the atmosphere can really called a problem. There is today some disagreement about this issue, and the reader will be exposed to the different positions in this debate.

Sometimes disagreements focus on what, if anything, should be done about a specific event or trend that is perceived to be a problem. For example, while acid rain is generally seen as a problem, various people disagree about what public policy actions would be appropriate to address this problem. Sometimes disagreements revolve around how specific action should be implemented. For example, while many people agree that actions should be taken to reduce air pollution, there is often disagreement about the best way to implement air pollution controls. In short, this book investigates a variety of environmental issues that have been, and probably will continue to be, controversial.

Before embarking on such an investigation, however, a quick review of some elements of the context in which environmental controversies develop in the United States might be in order. First, it is necessary to review the range of specific environmental problems or issues that are often identified as posing intermediate or potential threats. These "threats to environmental quality" should be examined because they obviously serve as the basis for understanding some of the policy alternatives and actions discussed later. Second, it might be useful to become familiar with the value bases of many environmental controversies. The argument here is that many of the disagreements that constitute environmental policy controversies are rooted in rather disparate values. So the underlying values or fundamental beliefs that seem to recur as roots of specific environmental disagreements are discussed.

Third, an examination of the state of public opinion about the environment can help provide a clear picture of how the general American public sees this issue. This public opinion information is used to help build an understanding of the contextual role played by opinions of the general public, and to provide a glimpse of the public opinion roots of many environmental controversies. This public opinion information is also used as an entrée to some of the debates that have arisen over the interpretation of the public's opinion. Ultimately, the result of reviewing this information is the development of some understanding as to what, if anything, existing information on public environmental opinion has to say about the public's concern for environmental issues and environmental protection.

Threats to Environmental Quality

Before taking a look at specific controversies about public environmental policy, it is necessary to review what some people have argued are major threats to the quality of our physical environment. For the most part, these threats (and later discussion of public policies) are subdivided according to the physical medium (air, water, soil, and so on) involved. No effort will be made in this chapter to try to review the evolution of public policy toward each of these threats—this is done in subsequent chapters. The purpose of the following materials simply is to explain the basic nature of specific threats to environmental quality. Public policies toward the environment aside for the moment, there are still quite a number of controversies surrounding the very definition of what constitutes an environmental threat.

The Air People Breathe

Air pollution has been an emerging and recurring problem in the United States for at least the past 30 years. Many people consider air pollution to be a problem by itself and, as will be seen shortly, it is thought to be a major contributor to acid rain, global warming, and perhaps other environmental problems. So air pollution is considered a problem for two major reasons: First, it is thought to cause direct health consequences; and second, it causes other problems that in turn create health consequences.

Air pollution comes from at least three major sources and many minor ones. The three major sources are: manufacturing and electric power generating industries; automobile exhaust; and naturally occurring substances such as radon gas. In general, the burning of fossil fuels as a source of energy produces substantial air pollution. There are many other sources of air pollution, including emissions from gasoline service station pumps, dry cleaners, backyard barbecues, and even livestock.

Air pollution is considered by many people to be a problem for several reasons. First, in severe cases, the quality of air has deteriorated to the point where people have suffered direct and immediate consequences. In the 1960s, during periods of air inversions in Pittsburgh and other cities, for example, citizens were often warned not to venture outside. In Southern California and many other places around the country today, the air is frequently considered unhealthful. For people already suffering from respiratory problems such as emphysema and asthma, this poor air quality can constitute very real and immediate health threats. But air pollution has other consequences as well.

The Problem of Acid Rain

Recently sulfur oxide and nitrogen oxide emissions from coal-burning electric power generating plants and nonferrous metal smelting factories, largely in the Midwest, have been linked to the creation of acid rain, a phenomenon whereby the natural rain that falls is extremely acidic. Acid rain is actually a specific form of a phenomenon generally known as acid deposition. Acidic water vapor in the atmosphere may return to the Earth as rain, snow, fog, or even acidified particulate matter. This acid deposition is thought to contribute to physical environments where plants and animals cannot live or cannot thrive, and many ecosystems have apparently been endangered from highly acidic water and soil. Many forests have suffered severe loss of trees, and many lakes and streams have suffered loss of fish and supporting plant populations. So the apparent consequences of some types of air pollution extend to other media, especially water and soil.

While newspapers and television have publicized the problem of acid rain, many people are not convinced that it is a serious problem, or that it is a problem with a single known cause. Still others disagree about whether acid rain actually produces damage to the environment. Chapter 3 makes it clear that there are many debates about what kinds of action government should take in response to various types of air pollution, including acid rain. Here, however, the focus is on the debates around whether acid rain is a problem, if so, what causes it, and what kinds of damage acid rain causes to the environment.

Is Acid Rain Really a Problem? Few people would argue that highly acidic rain is not an environmental problem. Occasionally one might hear of someone begrudgingly acknowledging an acid rain problem by suggesting that it can be solved quite easily. But even these people seem to agree that acid rain is, to some degree, a problem. Somewhat more debate exists about whether acid rain is an *increasing* problem, that is, whether it is getting worse. This debate suggests that if acid rain is an increasing problem, then a compelling case can be made for immediate public policy intervention. On the other hand, if acid rain is a phenomenon that is stable and not getting worse, the implication is that government intervention is premature since there is plenty of time to study and understand the problem. If acid rain is not getting appreciably worse, then is there an immediate need to take actions to combat it? Much of the debate about acid rain turns on what its causes are and what kinds of effects it has on the environment (Howard & Perley, 1980).

Does Air Pollution Cause Acid Rain? Even among those who seem to agree that acid rain does constitute an increasing problem, there is some disagreement as to what causes it. As noted earlier, increasing evidence indicates acid rain is the product of a highly complex set of chemical and meteorological reactions that take place in the Earth's atmosphere. Scientists have accounted for what they believe is one major catalyst for acid rain to occur and get worse: the use of very tall smokestacks on manufacturing plants.

The chemical reactions in the atmosphere start with large amounts of sulfur and nitrogen oxide being emitted into the air from manufacturing and electric generating facilities, especially those found in the East and the midwestern states of Ohio, Illinois, and Indiana, which tend to rely heavily on burning high sulfur coal as a fuel. As already noted, during the 1960s air pollution became a major problem. In response, Congress passed the Clean Air Act Amendments of 1970, implementation of which, among other things, sought to reduce local ambient air pollution by allowing polluting industries to install very tall smokestacks. These tall smokestacks appear to have simply transferred the pollution problem from the local area to areas far downwind. Because of the prevailing wind patterns and other meteorological events, high airborne pollutants from the Midwest make their way toward the northeastern United States and southeastern Canada.

Perhaps ironically, the tall smokestacks appear to have helped transport the sulfur and nitrogen oxide emissions to a level of the atmosphere where the requisite chemical reactions are more prolific and more likely to occur. This process produces sulfuric and nitric acids, which then combine with water vapor and fall to Earth as acid precipitation (Gorham, 1982). Thus for some, being able to account for the chemical processes provides a convincing case that specific industries create acid rain.

Other people are not convinced of the causes of acid rain. They suggest that because the detailed nature of the chemical reaction that would have to take place in the atmosphere is not fully known or understood, it cannot be said that airborne emissions cause or even contribute to acid rain. Moreover, there are those who claim that while emissions may create acid rain, this accounts for only a small amount of the acidity found in the environment (Brown, 1984). As will be discussed in Chapter 3, this position was adopted by the Reagan administration during the 1980s to justify conducting research rather than trying to control air pollution directly.

Probably the first detailed review of scientific studies on the causes of acid rain was presented in 1981 by the National Academy of Sciences, an association made up of some of the world's most prestigious scientists. This report examined and summarized numerous studies in an effort to make a reasoned judgment about the causes of acid rain, and it produced some compelling evidence that indeed airborne sulfur and nitrogen oxides do cause acid rain. However, the report also seems to have produced less-compelling evidence on whether acid rain actually harms the environment.

More recently, the National Acid Precipitation Assessment Program (NAPAP), a federal interagency task force, issued a comprehensive review of scientific studies conducted since 1980, including some of its own. The NAPAP was created by Congress in 1980 through enactment of the Energy Security Act, at least partially in response to the lack of definitive knowledge about the causes and consequences of acid rain. This Act created a federal interagency task force, composed of officials from the Environmental Protection Agency, the National Oceanic and Atmospheric Administration, the Departments of Energy, Agriculture, Interior, Health and Human Services, Commerce, and State, as well as a number of other agencies. This interagency task force then created the NAPAP to investigate acid rain over a 10-year period. In late 1990 the NAPAP issued its first integrated findings, which provide additional evidence that air pollution does indeed contribute to the problem of acid rain. While these findings acknowledge that many aspects of the relationship between air pollution and acid rain are still not completely known, the report also concludes that the linkage is clear enough to warrant efforts at reducing air pollution emissions (NAPAP, 1990).

Does Acid Rain Damage the Environment? Even among those who seem to agree that acid rain exists, and that it may very well be caused by air pollution, there is still debate about whether acid rain causes other environmental problems. Indeed, much of the reason why acid rain is thought to be a problem hinges on a finding that acid rain causes damage to other parts of the environment. Many concede that acid rain exists and that it may well be created by the combination of events described above, but they argue that it has not been the leading cause of other environmental damage often attributed to acid rain.

The main issue is whether acid rain is the principal cause of high levels of acidity in ground and surface water in the northeastern part of the United States. William Brown (1984, p. 173), the Director of Technological Studies at the Hoover Institute, has argued that acid rain is not responsible for the environmental damage often attributed to it. He argues that:

> [T]he pollutants in the rain are only a minor contributor to the high-level acidity found in some eastern lakes and streams. . . . this acidity, which is indeed hostile to the existence of game fish and other aquatic creatures, is mostly natural rather than industrial in origin. . . . [and] . . . the popular notion that acid rain is threatening forests in the eastern U.S., and indeed

all across the Temperate Zone, is based less on substance than upon ill-informed conjecture and is probably wrong.

Brown's argument, which he admits is a "minority view," is that most of the acidity found in surface water comes from the *mor humus*, or layers of organic material that build up on the floor of forests; as rain water passes through these layers, it picks up much more acid (perhaps 1,000 times as much acid) than that found in the rainwater itself. Further, he suggests that prevention of forest fires has had the secondary effect of eliminating a natural mechanism through which such acidity is often neutralized. Forest fires apparently burn the *mor humus,* reducing its acidity and replacing it with a layer of alkaline ash. Fires in forests adjacent to surface water bodies, then, are seen as an often naturally occurring mechanism through which groundwater acid is neutralized. When such fires are prevented, the naturally occurring acid is once again free to build up.

Subsequent analysis casts serious doubts on the arguments put forth by Brown. Much research reviewed in 1981 by the National Research Council and reported in 1990 by the National Acid Precipitation Assessment Program (NAPAP) has reinforced the initial argument that acid rain does indeed account for much of the acidity in lakes, rivers, and streams in parts of the United States (Johnson, 1986; NAPAP, 1990; National Research Council, 1986a: Rahn & Lowenthal, 1986). In late 1990 the NAPAP report provided some additional evidence that acid rain clearly causes environmental degradation. The report reviewed the surface water monitoring activities of its National Surface Water Survey and concluded that some 75% of acidic lakes and 50% of acidic streams were acidic because of acid rain (NAPAP, 1990, pp. 5-6). It also suggested that acid rain contributes significantly to forest damage, especially among red spruce trees at higher elevations; acid rain also causes damage to buildings and construction materials.

Even though there is clear evidence of the environmental consequences of acid rain as caused by air pollution, and good reason to believe that sulfur dioxide and other forms of air pollution contribute significantly to the problem of acid rain, and evidence that reducing air pollution would diminish the negative effects from acid rain, there is still much disagreement over whether the problem is serious enough to warrant potentially costly federal and state efforts to regulate air pollution emissions. Chapter 3 presents the case made by people who believe that controlling sulfur dioxide emissions is too expensive and harms the nation's economy too much. In their view, regulating and limiting air pollution is not cost-effective.

Air Pollution and Global Warming: The Greenhouse Effect

Acid rain is not the only problem associated with air pollution. Another well-publicized environmental problem thought to be related to air pollution is global warming, or the greenhouse effect (Bernard, 1980; MacDonald, 1988; Schneider, 1989). The greenhouse effect describes a situation in which air pollution collects in the Earth's atmosphere and subsequently causes that atmosphere's temperature to gradually increase. The result is that the Earth's climate warms and then causes a variety of other problems, such as increased melting of the polar ice caps. Ultimately, this would result in massive increases in the size of the Earth's oceans and commensurate decreases in land area.

Not everyone agrees that there is a problem of global warming. Some people suggest that, while it might be possible for air pollution to create the greenhouse effect, there is very little evidence that such warming has taken place, arguing that small fluctuations in average temperatures from year to year are natural and do not necessarily represent any long-term or permanent trend toward higher climactic temperatures. Yet as shown in Figure 1.1, there does seem to be a long-term trend toward global warming. This Figure shows that while there are indeed considerable short-term fluctuations in temperature, there is also a longer-term upward trend.

Additionally, global warming skeptics suggest that from a scientific perspective, it is possible to account for ways in which any of the purported air pollution causes of the greenhouse effect might be neutralized through naturally occurring processes. In other words, it is possible to show that for every potential cause of the greenhouse effect, there might be naturally occurring processes that prevent the greenhouse effect from actually taking place. The following examination of how and why the greenhouse effect has come to be considered a problem might help in understanding this debate.

The problem of global warming, or the greenhouse effect, is thought to be a product of air pollution. The idea is not that complex. Global warming is thought to be caused by air pollution in the form of carbon dioxide (from burning fossil fuels, especially automobile exhaust), methane (mostly from cattle), and nitrous oxide and chlorofluoro-

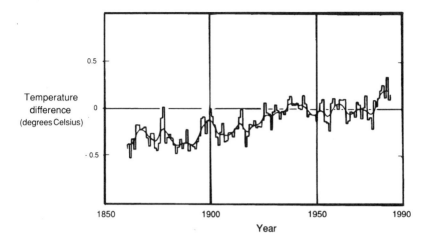

Figure 1.1. Average Annual Temperature Variations Since 1861

SOURCE: From "Global Temperature Variation Between 1861 and 1984" by P. Jones, T. Wigley, and P. Wright, 1986, reprinted by permission from *Nature* vol. 322, pp. 430-434; Copyright © 1986 Macmillan Magazines Limited.

carbons (from industrial manufacturing) collecting in the Earth's upper atmosphere. These gases are largely the result of pollution from manufacturing industries, agriculture, automobiles, and household products. As these gases collect in the atmosphere, they do two things: They let in the sun's warming rays; and they act as insulators preventing excess heat from escaping the atmosphere. As a result, average global temperatures have probably been increasing for some time.

There are a number of serious consequences to this global warming. As mentioned earlier, one consequence is the rapid melting of the polar ice caps, which would result in both a substantial increase in the size of the Earth's oceans and a commensurate decrease in the amount of exposed land area. In many scenarios, global warming is capable of changing the entire shape of all of the world's continents, presumably producing serious hardship for populations residing in those areas most affected. For example, Figure 1.2 provides one picture of what the eastern part of the United States might look like as a result of polar ice cap melting. The gray shading represents areas that would be covered by water. According to this projection, nearly the entire states of Florida and Louisiana would be covered by water. But decreased land area is not the only consequence.

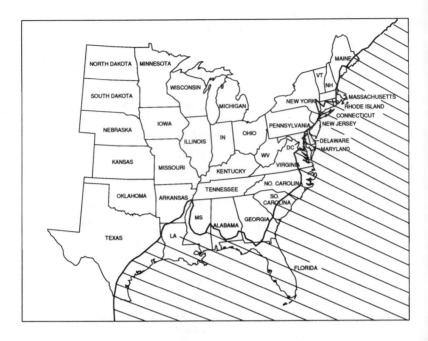

Figure 1.2. Projected Impacts of Global Warming

SOURCE: From *Ice Age Lost* (p. 301) (based on information from U.S. Geological Survey) by G. Schultz, 1974. New York: Anchor Press/Doubleday. Copyright 1974 by G. Schultz. Reprinted by permission.

According to various climate models, increases in global temperatures would mean considerably greater rainfall (National Academy of Sciences, 1983). However, this rainfall would not be evenly distributed, and might even result in a redistribution of rainfall such that centers of continents at middle latitudes, including the midwestern United States, would suffer persistent drought. Additionally, there is evidence that increased temperatures usually result in an increase in the number and species of insects. Agricultural production would then face greater problems of pest control. Even though many people seem to believe that the world would simply adapt to whatever changes might take place, there is increasing reason to believe that such adaptations would be very difficult (Mintzer, 1988; Revkin, 1988).

*Air Pollution and Depletion
of the Earth's Ozone Layer*

The Earth has layers of atmosphere, and each layer's chemical composition is quite different. One of these layers, the stratosphere, is composed of gases including ozone. This ozone layer of the atmosphere plays a significant role in protecting most of the living creatures of the world from the potentially harmful ultraviolet portion of the sun's rays. The ozone in the stratosphere actually filters out these harmful rays and prevents them from reaching the planet's surface. Thus, people and other living organisms are not exposed to most of these rays. The most immediate threat to humans from depletion of the ozone layer comes in the form of increased skin cancer and cataracts from exposure to the sun's damaging rays.

Air pollution threatens to decrease the protection offered by the ozone layer. Certain types of air pollutants, especially those collectively referred to as chlorofluorocarbons, are capable of depleting this ozone layer. Chlorofluorocarbons (CFCs) are gases—some of the same chemicals earlier identified as being among those responsible for the greenhouse effect—frequently used in manufacturing many household and industrial products. CFCs have been used as propellants to make aerosol cans work (cans containing hairspray, spray paint, and so on), although this use has been banned in the United States since the mid-1970s. A widely used man-made CFC, freon, makes air conditioners work. Still other such gases are used in the production of polystyrene or styrofoam, a material used for foam insulation, coffee cups, package padding, and many other products. As these gases are released into the atmosphere during or after the production of various products, they gradually collect in the Earth's upper atmosphere, where they apparently do their damage.

It was not until about 1974 that scientific evidence established that chlorofluorocarbons potentially threaten the Earth's atmosphere (Molina & Rowland, 1974). There is now significant evidence that these released CFCs have been responsible for a general thinning of the ozone layer of the atmosphere (Cohn, 1987; Graedel & Crutzen, 1989). Additionally, much scientific attention has been focused on holes in this layer, especially over Antarctica (the South Pole). Although the precise chemical reactions that might be causing the depletion of the ozone layer are not fully understood, it seems clear that the depletion has paralleled the increased use of CFCs. Because the scientific evidence is not complete, many people again argue that it is premature for governments to consider taking actions that could potentially harm economic development. Even so, some 35 countries signed, and at least 14 nations have ratified, the 1987 Montreal Protocol, a multinational agreement to phase out and control the use of these chemicals.

The Water People Drink and Use

Just as many people consider air pollution to be a serious problem, so too do many believe that water pollution constitutes a major threat to our way of life. Over the past 20 years, water pollution has come to be perceived by many as among the most serious of all threats to human existence (Postel, 1986). Increasingly, private home owners and municipal governments are finding that their well water contains hazardous pollutants. Many lakes, streams, oceans, and other waterways have become so severely polluted that they no longer can be used for either recreation or consumption (Smith, Alexander, & Wolman, 1987). The oceans have become apparently convenient, albeit illegal, dumping grounds for a variety of materials that are difficult to dispose of, including contaminated medical waste. Seeing used syringes washed up on the beaches of New Jersey and New York has helped drive home the point that water pollution is indeed a widespread problem.

While a considerable amount of water pollution is apparently the result of acid rain, other major forms of water pollution come from a variety of sources, including the improper or illegal disposal of hazardous wastes; the overuse and abuse of pesticides, insecticides, herbicides, and other products in agriculture and home lawn care; accidental discharges of hazardous materials, such as oil spills, leaking gasoline storage tanks; and the improper or inadequate treatment and disposal of municipal and private sewage. Many areas used for fishing, and harvesting clams and other seafood, have become restricted because the seafood contains toxic levels of bacteria from either unprocessed or underprocessed sewage.

Aside from the previously cited debate over acid rain's contribution to water pollution, few people would argue about whether water pollution is a problem. Chapters 4 and 5 present the idea that there are many who acknowledge that water pollution is a problem but dispute what, if anything, should be done by government, especially the federal government, about it (Congressional Digest, 1985). These chapters will also present an introduction to the debates about whether, to what extent, and in what ways government should be involved with making decisions about these water pollution and water usage issues.

Polluting the Land: Toxic and Hazardous Waste

As already noted, contaminated soil is a major source of water pollution. The contamination of the land has also become a major environmental problem in its own right. Perhaps the most widely recognized problem over the past 10 years, polluted land has emerged as a problem in at least three related ways. First, partly through the implementation of the Superfund program, which is discussed in Chapter 5, people have become increasingly aware of the numerous hazardous waste sites that have been discovered around the country. Second, as a result of efforts to prevent the development of future hazardous waste sites through regulating the disposal of solid, hazardous, and toxic wastes, it has become increasingly difficult to find places to dispose of household and industrial trash. And third, as the available landfill space has decreased, the cost of disposing of solid wastes has increased dramatically. This has led to efforts to site new disposal facilities, and these siting efforts themselves often produce considerable local controversy. The nation's public policies toward toxic and hazardous waste are numerous and address these problems in a variety of ways. Federal and state efforts to create an effective hazardous and toxic waste pollution policy are discussed in Chapter 5.

The Clash of Underlying Values
in Environmental Attitudes

Having looked at some contemporary debates and controversies about environmental problems, we can now turn to some of the root foundations that frequently underlie these controversies. Disagreements of the sort described earlier, and to be described later, are often the product of clashes of values, which means that people often disagree over what should be valued in society, bringing into play the many attitudes and beliefs that cause these disputes to flourish. There are five different types of clashes elaborated here, involving:

- The values of science and technology versus humanism;
- The values of economics (especially efficiency) versus humanism;
- The role of nature in society;
- The role of government in society; and
- Science, technology, and economics versus the practice of politics.

Before we use these clashes in an effort to understand something about environmental controversies, a brief explanation and some examples are in order.

The Clash of Science and Technology Versus Humanism

One of the most prominent normative underpinnings of many environmental disagreements can be traced to different perceptions of the proper relationship between technology and society. Should science and technology be the driving force behind social innovation? Or should society, treating issues through a more humanistic approach, dictate the bounds of what science and technology attempt to do? Stated another way, should scientists have a free rein to determine the directions of society, or should society use science only for those purposes deemed desirable in their own right? This is a question that has persisted in many different contexts for generations.

There have been numerous exposés of the clash of these two perspectives, but none has expressed this type of value duality more clearly than that found in the works of the novelist C. P. Snow (1960, 1964). Snow describes the fundamental difficulties inherent in mutual understanding between what he calls "scientists" and "humanists." To Snow, difficulties in reaching such a mutual understanding flow from the fact that these groups speak very different languages. Scientists are acculturated into a set of beliefs and normative prescriptions about the role of science in society, about the proper way to conduct scientific inquiry, and about the value of the results of scientific inquiry to society. Humanists, on the other hand, tend to reject many of the beliefs and normative underpinnings of science, instead preferring to emphasize the need to humanize, subjectify, and contextualize each decision under consideration. Humanists tend to see science not as providing final answers to social problems, but rather as displacing problems—that is creating new problems by shifting them to someone else, someplace else, or sometime in the future (Dryzek, 1987).

In elaborating the ways that this clash of cultures as paradigms affects environmental decisions, Cotgrove (1982) explains:

> It is because protagonists to the debate approach issues from different culture contexts, which generate different and conflicting implicit meanings, that there is mutual exasperation and charges and countercharges of irrationality and unreason. What is sensible from one point of view is nonsense from another. It is the implicit, self-evident, taken-for-granted character of paradigms which clogs the channels of communication. (p. 82)

This clash of cultures often appears to manifest itself in many environmental controversies. For example, the clash of these cultures frequently results from differing ideas about the risks that society should bear from the development and use of various environmentally impacting technologies. The scientific approach to risks relies on given standards and methodologies applied in an "objective" fashion. The idea is that the level and type of environmental risk posed by a particular technology can be estimated through rigorous quantification and measurement, and adherence to the scientific method. As a result, the scientific approaches to environmental risk lend themselves to the development of unique, detailed, and very technical language and concepts that one might suggest come close to constituting a culture (Dietz & Rycroft, 1987).

The scientific approach to risks purposely avoids discussion of value positions until the level and type of risk are objectively estimated. This scientific approach suggests that once estimated, the environmental risk can be evaluated subjectively to decide whether it is worthwhile bearing, avoiding, or changing through purposeful actions. (Morone & Woodhouse, 1986; Wilson & Crouch, 1987) Indeed, Kraft and Vig (1988) suggest that this constitutes something of an instrumental view of science and technology, where technology is thought of as being value-neutral. According to this view, it is the purposes and uses of science and technology as decided by humans that determine whether that technology is something to be positively or negatively valued. This view of the role of environmental risk has become so dominant that the EPA now advocates incorporation of scientific risk analysis in nearly all public environmental decisions (USEPA, 1990).

To the humanist, however, the estimation of environmental risk cannot be accomplished in such a neat and clean value-free way. The humanist tends to see the scientific approach and associated methodologies as being rather limited forms of human expression, and also tends to feel the need to consider the broader range of human concerns about a given risk from the outset. To the humanist, the scientist's value-neutral analysis is a myth—instead of being value-free, scientific methodologies carry with them implicit values at all levels (Wynne, 1982).

Although it may be something of an oversimplification to aggregate those alternative views under the rubric "humanism," it does capture at least one element of an important source of controversy in many environmental decisions. Although numerous examples of this type of clash are presented in subsequent chapters, there is one example that can be described here to illustrate this clash of values.

One can see what seem to be clear elements of this clash reflected in many environmental decisions, such as decisions as to where to site hazardous waste treatment facilities, created in an effort to diminish the flow of hazardous wastes into landfills or dumps. For many people, decisions to site facilities constitute clashes between "experts," who want to site a facility in a specific location based on objective analysis, and the "public," which does not want it there. People who live in the affected community tend to take on decidedly humanist roles, often arguing that the experts could not have conducted value-free assessments of the risks and other characteristics of the particular site. These residents often believe implicitly that the scientific analysis does not reflect an understanding of their community or their way of life. Consequently, the public tends to distrust the experts, and to believe that experts' conclusions are seriously flawed. Usually this clash of values makes siting facilities next to impossible (Portney, 1991a).

The experts, on the other hand, often perceive that they are conducting the best possible analysis of the risks and costs associated with the specific site. In their minds, the public is totally irrational in its opposition to the facility. Their feeling is that if the public could only be made to understand the rational way they made their determination, then opposition would subside. The point is that one or both parties in such conflicts exhibit rather strict adherence to the idea that they are correct and the other is incorrect, and that such strict adherence is rooted in deep differences of opinion of what should be valued. Consequently, both parties end up unable to communicate and subsequently resolve their differences.

The Clash of Economic Efficiency Versus Humanism

Just as disputes frequently contain elements of the clash between the values of science versus humanism, so too do they contain elements of a clash between economic efficiency and humanism. This clash boils down to one central theme: Should the pursuit of economic efficiency, especially through the operation of free and open markets, take precedence over protection of life? Or should the operation of the economic marketplace be guided foremost by what is good for the protection of life? Stated more succinctly, should the earth's resources be used in the name of efficient economic development even if to do so might cause human suffering, or should economic development be constrained to preclude harm to mankind?

To many economists, the pursuit of economic efficiency is the very mechanism through which the human condition is improved. So the pursuit of economic efficiency, by its very nature, is considered beneficial to society. However, many events over the past 20 years have convinced some people that this is not necessarily so. Oil spills in the gulfs of Alaska and Mexico, the accident at the nuclear-powered electric generating plant at Three Mile Island, and other events, raise serious questions about whether the pursuit of economic development and efficiency automatically produces the most beneficial results for humankind.

The clash of economics versus humanism takes another related form as well. In this form, environmental protection (as a humanist value) is pitted against the need for expanded employment opportunities. This clash pits environmental protection against jobs. However, proponents of environmental protection rarely concede that jobs must be lost in order to create a cleaner environment. To environmentalists, the task of cleaning and maintaining a clean environment, if it were highly valued in society, would more than compensate for the loss of jobs from abandoning currently polluting economic development. On the other side, advocates of economic development rarely concede that environmental protection values are truly humanistic. Proponents of economic development and efficiency, once again, view the production of goods and services as providing the greatest service to humankind. Whether overt efforts at environmental protection are more humanistic than efforts at stimulating the economy is a debate which will not be resolved any time soon. This clash between economics and humanism also finds its way into the clash between science and economics versus politics, as will be discussed shortly. Yet, this clash of values between economic efficiency and humanism also has implications for the prescribed role of nature in our society.

The Clash of Beliefs About the Role
of Nature in Society

Perhaps an even more deeply rooted clash of values than those already discussed can be found in the prescribed relationship between nature and society, or between the physical environment and the people who inhabit that environment. The type of relationship between nature and society one values carries with it inevitable links to economic issues. The issue is one of whether society's principal role, even obligation, is to conserve and protect the environment, or rather to economically exploit the environment for the benefit of humankind. There are clear traditions in American culture to support both positions (Buttel & Flinn, 1976; 1977).

Both positions can be traced to spiritual components of the Judeo-Christian tradition in America. In each position, the tradition starts with the belief in human dominion over the Earth and its other living creatures. But this is about as far as the common tradition goes. The positions diverge in their interpretation of what "dominion" actually means. To the environmental conservationist, the idea of dominion compares to St. Francis of Assisi's notion of human stewardship of all God's creatures. To someone like Lynn White, this means that nature should be valued for its own sake, and therefore people have a duty to protect nature from assaults resulting from economic market exploitation (White, 1967). To Ophuls (1977), the issue is one of protecting the environment for the survival of humankind.

To today's advocates of free markets in the economy, the idea of dominion engenders a very different, perhaps even opposite, meaning. To them, the idea of dominion means that nature and its environment should be used in the service of society, directly toward the goal of bettering God's earthly kingdom. Consequently, these people often feel that they have an obligation to use the Earth's resources and economically exploit them for the betterment of humankind. Thus, these diametrically opposed definitions of dominion set the normative stage for specific clashes over environmental decisions.

As it applies to environmental issues, Lester Milbrath argues that the advocates of free-market approaches and proponents of the use of nature in the service of humankind are adherents to what he calls the "dominant social paradigm" (Milbrath, 1984). He refers to these people as the environmental "rearguard" because they are defenders of this dominant social paradigm. On the other hand, he suggests that people who challenge this dominant social paradigm constitute the environmental "vanguard."

Equally important, Milbrath presents empirical information from a three-nation study (the United States, England, and West Germany), showing that these two distinctly different groups exist in all three nations, and that the vanguard possesses distinctly different values from the rearguard. The compelling evidence is that the vanguard does indeed believe in protecting the Earth's resources in their own right and from assaults perpetrated in the name of economic efficiency or improvement. Unlike the rearguard, the vanguard rejects the idea that the Earth should be used in service to mankind. As will be seen in the examination of public opinion toward the environment, not everyone fits into these two groups, and the vast majority of people adhere to tenets of both. Milbrath's argument, however, is that social change toward adopting more of the vanguard's values will be necessary for the survival of the planet.

The manifestation of this set of value conflicts can be seen in people's attitudes toward a variety of environmental controversies. Again, there are many examples of this clash of values in subsequent chapters. However, elements of this clash are clearly reflected in people's attitudes toward some environmental risks. Milbrath argues that adherents to the dominant social paradigm, with their "exuberant role toward nature in a competitive market system, urge humans to accept risk in order to maximize wealth." Members of the vanguard "have much greater reservations [about accepting risk] and would proceed with more caution" (p. 30).

On its face, at least, it appears that members of the rearguard possess a much higher level of environmental risk acceptance than do members of the vanguard. For example, adherents to rearguard values might be more willing to accept the risks of building and using nuclear electric power generating facilities than members of the vanguard. This risk acceptance presumably flows from the belief that the potential environmental damage produced by a nuclear accident and the actual damage produced by nuclear waste constitute reasonable prices to pay for the economic benefits provided by the electricity produced. Members of the vanguard would probably be much less accepting of the risks, largely because they are less inclined to believe that one must accept threats to the environment in order to obtain necessary economic benefits, or the economic benefits are not as highly valued in the first place.

The Clash Over the Role of Government in Society

Political theorists have long attempted to formulate prescriptions about the proper relationship between government and the individuals who compose society. Two competing conceptions of this relationship capture the breadth of difference manifest in contemporary American society. One of these is the concept of "individualism"; the other is the value of "communitarianism" (Bellah, Madsen, Sullivan, Swidler, & Tipton, 1985; Tocqueville, 1964). Individualism emphasizes the rights of people to do as they please, with little constraint from government. It finds its most prevalent manifestation through the assertion of individual property rights. Communitarianism emphasizes social utility and finds its basis in assertions of what is good for public health, safety, and social welfare.

In normative prescriptions emphasizing individualism, government is said to be best when it governs the least. Where communitarianism is emphasized, government's role is said to be to protect the public good and to prevent the exercise of individual rights that have the effect of doing violence to public health, safety, or welfare. These central and competing values find their way into many environmental conflicts.

First, the value of individualism as manifest in property rights itself serves as the basis for conflict. This type of clash is present in many disagreements related to business development. For example, a business may own a piece of land, and the officers of that business may decide they want to make some use of that land in order to increase profits and be more competitive in the economic marketplace. Inescapably, using the land has environmental impacts or implications. One could argue that this type of situation is an extension of the clash of values over the role of nature in society or the clash of economics versus politics. But there is an additional clash of values between individual versus communitarian rights.

A business might assert its basic right to develop a piece of property by virtue of the implicit property rights it has in owning the land, even if it causes some environmental damage. Of course, this claim to a right gives way to the realities of government regulation, where at least one administrative agency invariably must approve the property development. The agency, usually acting on behalf of communitarian values of protecting the health and welfare of the larger society, may take exception to the proposed development. Frequently, developers who adhere to the values of individualism reject the right of an agency to interfere with their property rights. Adherents to these values of individualism often reject the notion that communitarian values have a place in American society.

Taken separately or together, these clashes of values constitute the major foundations for the vast majority of environmental controversies in the United States. The ways these value clashes underlie environmental issues is the subject of later chapters; however, a description of some ways they work their way into American politics might be in order.

Science, Technology, and Economics Versus the Practice of Politics: Manifestations of Value Clashes

Almost inevitably, such deeply rooted value differences find their way into the arena of politics and public policy-making. The value differences already described often prescribe very different courses of action for public decision makers. Frequently, these courses of action conflict with one another—one cannot be undertaken without violating the goals of another. Sometimes these clashes manifest themselves more in federal or national politics, sometimes more in state or local politics. Here several short examples reveal how some of these clashes tend to manifest themselves in our political system.

Strong elements of the clash of economic efficiency versus humanism are often present in debate on whether government ought to take explicit action on behalf of the environment, for example, to enact stricter air pollution laws or to adopt most any other type of environmental regulation. Environmental regulations are not opposed just on the basis of economic considerations; many of the debates about environmental protection carry other value-based arguments as well. But the threat of the loss of jobs motivates much opposition to stricter environmental protection. Many people have opposed further reductions in automobile exhaust emissions, for example, because such reductions might hurt the American auto industry. Regulations allowing for large fines or financial penalties for improper disposal of toxic wastes have been opposed because these regulations would increase the costs of producing various products. Government efforts to require power plants in the Midwest to switch to low-sulfur coal have been resisted because much of our domestic coal is high-sulfur, and because those employed in many coal mines would presumably be displaced from their jobs. The timber industry in the Pacific Northwest opposed efforts to protect forests, including old-growth forests, because livelihoods depend on harvesting

such timber. Aside from carrying the clash of economics versus humanism into public policy-making, these debates also reflect the more
traditional clash between ideological conservatives and liberals.

Concern over the economic impact of environmental regulation often
suggests that humanists (sometimes mistakenly equated with ideological liberals) cannot reasonably justify protecting the environment at all
costs. Tolley, Graves, and Blomquist (1981, p. 19) offer this point of
view when they say that:

> The wholly justifiable concern that the environment may be neglected in
> private decisions suggests that there are crucial trade-offs that it is worth-
> while to make through public policy. However, the concern does not
> justify the . . . position that environmental action to abate pollution should be
> taken without weighing the advantages and disadvantages. It is abun-
> dantly clear that the value of numerous aspects of the environment is far
> less than infinite. Few people would live in burlap forever to get five more
> miles of visibility, and few people would exist at starvation levels to get
> pure water. It follows that comparisons [of alternative courses of action]
> are inevitable and weights are needed.

Many other examples of these value conflicts are represented in later
chapters' descriptions of public policy controversies.

Public Opinion Toward the Environment
and Its Protection

Elements of these value differences are to be found among the general
population as well. In recent years, considerable efforts have been made
to investigate the general public's attitudes and opinions about the environment, partly with an eye toward anticipating how much public support
there is for public environmental regulation. In the process, much has been
learned about the character of public opinion toward the environment.

Levels of Public Concern and
Support for Environmental Protection

When people speak of public opinion, they are usually referring to
the results of scientifically conducted surveys or polls of national

samples of the American people. Although there are many other ways of judging public opinion, this is one of the few approaches designed to provide accurate (unbiased) results (Mitchell, 1980). It is, however, somewhat difficult to build a complete picture of public opinion about the environment for at least three reasons. First, many different environmentally related issues have been addressed by survey research through national samples of citizens. Opinions on one set of issues may look totally different from those on another set of issues. The way people view air pollution can be very different from the way they view water pollution or other issues.

Second, different survey research questions may emphasize different aspects of the same issues, sometimes producing what appear to be very different results. For example, if people are asked whether they are extremely concerned about the environment, perhaps as many as two-thirds say yes. However, when they have been asked to give the most important issue facing the country today, the environment has not fared very well. In a 1988 Gallup survey asking this type of question, the environment was the most important issue for only 4% of the population, while the federal deficit was most important for some 25%, unemployment for 14%, high taxes for 12%, and so on. Third, only two major national surveys have asked the same questions repeatedly over a period of many years. Thus, existing information provides only a glimpse of how public opinion seems to have changed over time.

In general, there is much evidence that the American public is very concerned about environmental issues and highly supportive of efforts to protect the environment. Almost all of the major public opinion surveys indicate that usually more than half of the American people want a cleaner and safer environment. Different surveys ask people different questions, but the general pattern seems consistent. For example, a 1988 Gallup Survey revealed that some 66% of the public feels "extremely concerned" about pollution of oceans and beaches, 66% is extremely concerned about pollution of drinking water, and 50% is concerned about air pollution.

This apparent concern for environment quality also seems to carry over to opinion about governmental policies. For example, in a 1982 Gallup survey, people were asked whether they favor or oppose a number of different proposals including "strict enforcement of air and water pollution controls as now required by Clean Air and Clean Water Acts." Some 83% of the public favored strict enforcement, more than favored not cutting Social Security, or even prohibiting the Justice

Department and federal courts from ordering busing to achieve social balance (Mitchell, 1984, p. 65). A 1986 American National Election Studies survey conducted by the Institute for Social Research at the University of Michigan asked people about federal spending on environmental protection. This survey showed that about 50.6% of the people surveyed felt that federal spending on improving and protecting the environment should be increased. Only about 4.6% felt that spending should be reduced. More recently, a Gallup survey focused on the 1988 presidential election revealed that having a president interested in "proposing new laws to increase protection of the environment" was a very high priority for a significant majority of people, second only to reducing the federal deficit.

What is less clear, however, is how much people are willing to pay for a cleaner environment, whether people feel the environment is among the most important problems in the United States or the world, and how persistent these attitudes are over time. The common wisdom is that people are generally in favor of environmental protection until they have to pay for it. Yet, according to Mitchell (1984, p. 52), the decade of the 1970s saw that " majorities—faced with trade-offs between protecting the environment and its possible costs, such as closing factories—consistently chose the environmental side."

The issue of trade-offs, as posited through survey research, must be examined very carefully (Francis, 1983). Ladd (1982) has argued that public opinion on trade-offs between economic growth and environmental protection can look very different, depending on the emphasis in the questions asked. He points to two surveys conducted in 1981, using different questions to assess peoples' positions on this trade-off issue. In the first, an ABC News/*Washington Post* poll, people were asked to agree or disagree with the idea that "some important regulations aimed at protecting the environment should be dropped so we can improve the economy." In response, 54% said they agree and 40% said they disagree, giving the clear impression that people tend to favor economic growth over environmental protection.

However, the second poll, a CBS News/*New York Times* survey, asked people to align themselves with one of two statements: (1) we need to relax our environmental laws in order to achieve economic growth; or (2) we need to maintain present environmental laws in order to preserve the environment for future generations. Some 21% of the people favored relaxing standards, while 67% favored maintaining them. Perhaps more important, Ladd notes that the majority of Americans seem to want both economic growth and a clean environment. Pointing to a 1981 survey by the Opinion Research Corporation, which asked people to identify which of three statements they most agreed with, some 59% said that they believed that "we can achieve our current national goals of environmental protection and business and new job growth at the same time"; while only 22% agreed with the statement that "we must relax environmental standards in order to achieve business and new job growth"; and only 15% said "we must accept a slower rate of business and new job growth in order to protect our environment." The point is that most people do not seem to readily accept the idea that there must be a trade-off between economic growth and environmental protection. This provides additional support for the idea that most people do not clearly possess either the "rearguard" or "vanguard" values described by Milbrath.

Thus, the strength of opinion about the environment appears to run fairly deep. In other words, people do not tend to back away from supporting environmental protection when faced with possible trade-offs. But before the impression is created that public opinion has been totally unvarying over a period of years, there are surveys providing additional insight into this issue.

Trends in Public Attitudes Over Time

As noted earlier, only two major series of surveys elicited the public's opinion on environmental issues by asking the same questions over time. Both of these series of surveys, the General Social Surveys and surveys conducted by the Roper organization, asked questions related to support for government efforts on environmental protection. From the first of these, as shown in Figure 1.3, public opinion toward governmental spending to clean up the environment has fluctuated between 1971 and 1988, the period during which the General Social Survey repeatedly asked the same question. In these surveys, respondents were asked whether they thought we are spending "too little," "too much," or "about the right amount" for the environment and environmental protection. Figure 1.3 strongly suggests that opinions indicating that government is spending "too little" have remained quite high over this entire period.

Starting in 1971 there appeared to be substantial support for spending more on environmental protection, but this support steadily eroded until about 1979 or 1980, around the time when Ronald Reagan was first

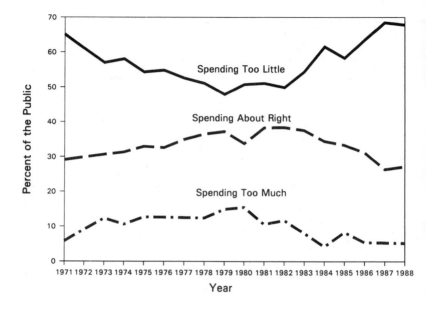

Figure 1.3. Public Opinion Toward Spending for Environmental Protection, 1971-1988

SOURCE: The General Social Surveys, as taken from Niemi, Mueller, and Smith, 1989, p. 79.

elected president. Then attitudes reflecting the desire to spend more on the environment started to build once again (Schneider, 1983). By 1987 and 1988 public opinion supporting environmental protection was at an all-time high for this entire period. Although this series of surveys is not perfectly up-to-date, there is independent reason to believe that public opinion remains highly supportive of efforts to protect the environment in the 1990s.

The same general tendency, at least between 1973 and 1981, is revealed in surveys conducted by the Roper organization. These results, as shown in Figure 1.4, reveal people's attitudes about whether they thought "environmental protection laws and regulations have gone too far, or not far enough, or have struck about the right balance." The figure reveals fairly strong sentiment that laws and regulations have struck the right balance or have not gone far enough. It also shows, consistent with the results from the General Social Surveys, that the percentage of the public saying that laws and regulations have gone too

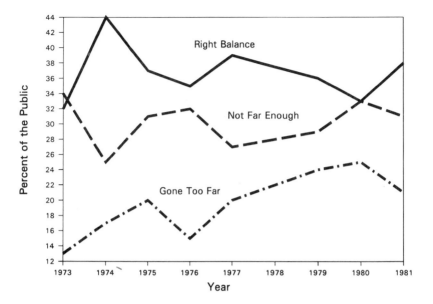

Figure 1.4. Public Opinion on Environmental Laws and Regulations, 1973-1981
SOURCE: Roper Organization surveys, as reported in *Public Opinion,* February/March 1982, p. 32.

far increased until about 1980. It would appear that support for environmental protection reached its low mark around 1980, although a feeling that environmental laws and regulations have not gone far enough also reached a peak at about that time. This may well be reflective of the attitude mobilizing effect that opposition to environmental policies had on the environmental movement (Mitchell, 1984, pp. 60-64).

It is not clear why there has been change in attitudes toward the environment over time. These trends upward or downward may be strongly influenced by the general state of the nation's economy and perceptions of national economic performance. This might be especially relevant for attitudes toward government spending on environmental protection. For example, as the nation's inflation reached double digits through the 1970s, people seemed to feel increasingly that too much or the right amount was being spent. As the economy improved during the 1980s, attitudes toward government spending turned around. This was not quite so clear in the case of attitudes toward environmental regulation, where there appears to have been somewhat more short-term fluctuation. There are alternative explanations; it is possible that when the federal government is perceived as being very active in protecting the environment, people increasingly begin to believe that perhaps enough has been accomplished. When the federal government is perceived as being relatively inactive on, or inattentive to, the environment, people begin to believe that more should be done. However, until systematic analysis is available, these explanations can only be speculative.

Another important question about public attitudes relates to electoral politics. Does the general strength of attitudes in favor of environmental protection necessarily have implications for electoral politics? Does support for environmental protection translate into support for candidates who favor environmental protection?

The Role of Environmental Attitudes in Elections

While these data provide a fairly clear idea of the range of public attitudes toward the environment and environmental policy, much less is known about the role these attitudes play in electoral outcomes (Lake, 1983). It has been suggested, for example, that because people are so supportive of environmental protection they might be influenced to seek out and elect candidates for public office who also support environmental protection. Whether this has happened is open to question, and was the subject of debate between two prominent survey researchers: Louis Harris, of Louis Harris and Associates, and Everett Carll Ladd, of the University of Connecticut.

Harris initiated the debate in the early 1980s, when he made the claim that environmental issues were so important to the American people that candidates would be elected or defeated on this issue alone. His initial claims were contained in testimony before the House Subcommittee on Health and the Environment, which was holding hearings in 1981 in consideration of a new Clean Air Act. According to Harris, public support for the existing Clean Air Act's provisions was so strong that any members of Congress who tried to weaken the Act would face the very real prospect of being defeated at their next elections. These views were repeated to the Environmental Industry Council in March of 1982, and were circulated around Washington by environmental interest groups.

One member of Congress, James Broyhill (R-North Carolina), concerned about the implications of Harris' contentions for his desire to seek modification to the Clean Air Act, solicited the views of Ladd, an experienced survey researcher at the University of Connecticut and an associate with the conservative Hoover Institute. Ladd had published an article in the journal *Public Opinion Quarterly* in which he criticized some of the inferences Harris drew about public opinion toward the environment.

Ladd provided Broyhill with a critique that soundly refuted Harris' interpretations, arguing that relatively few people would vote against a candidate with whom they disagreed on environmental protection. In other words, Ladd claimed that while many people support environmental protection, most do not feel so strongly about this one issue that they would vote against a candidate who was less supportive of the environment. In retrospect, very little evidence exists that public attitudes toward the environment played a very significant role in subsequent elections, whether national, state, or local.

Who Among the General Public Is Most Supportive of Environmental Protection?

These survey research results have built a fairly clear picture of the magnitude and depth of public opinion toward the environment, but there are some related questions that might help improve this picture. In particular, there has been some debate about who tends to be more supportive or less supportive of environmental protection (Buttel & Flinn, 1978a). Such debates have focused on two specific groups of people—women and people from upper-middle or upper-class backgrounds (Buttel & Flinn, 1978b). Examining these two issues will help create a more complete picture.

Is There a Gender Gap in Attitudes Toward the Environment? Are women more concerned about or more protective of the environment than men? Although many people argue that this is the case, research on this issue has produced mixed results. Studies by Catton and Dunlap (1978), Dunlap and Catton (1979), and McStay and Dunlap (1983) found that women tended to be more protective of, and more supportive of efforts to clean up, the environment than men. Analyses have also documented that women may be more likely than men to oppose the use, licensing, and siting of nuclear-power generating plants (Brody, 1984; Mitchell, 1984; Nealey, Melber, & Rankin, 1983; Passino & Lounsbury, 1976).

On the other hand, a review by Van Liere and Dunlap of studies conducted through 1980 concluded that there is no general pattern of gender-based differences. As they noted, "evidence regarding sex and [general] environmental concern is quite meager and the results [of studies] . . . are inconclusive" (1980, p. 191). And in a more recent study of attitudes toward acid rain, women seem to be less concerned than men (Arcury, Scollay, & Johnson, 1987). So there does not appear to be any sort of universal pattern for women to be more environmentally protective or concerned than men.

More recently, however, efforts have been made to uncover some ways in which men and women do seem to exhibit different attitudes about the environment. There seems to be a tendency for women to be more concerned about specific types of environmental issues—those that are in some way "local" in nature. For example, Brody (1984) found that when the issue was local use of nuclear power plants to generate electricity, women were more opposed than men. When the issue was general attitudes toward nuclear energy, there were only small differences between men and women. George and Southwell (1986) found that, among residents near the Diablo Canyon nuclear power plant in California, women were much more opposed than men to licensing this facility. All of these studies point to gender differences associated with local environmental issues or problems.

Assuming that there are gender differences on local environmental issues, it is somewhat difficult to know why such differences should exist. Brody's (1984) analysis ascribed disproportionate environmental concern among women to role socialization. This explanation suggests that women are socialized to have what are termed "nurturant and expressive" roles rather than "instrumental" ones. This line of inquiry stimulated several studies to investigate what the role of "motherhood" or having children might play in gender differences. Studies by Hamilton (1985a; 1985b) and Blocker and Eckberg (1989) suggest that women with children exhibit more environmental concern than women or men without children.

All of this seems to point to one central conclusion: While there does not seem to be an overall gender gap, there is a gender gap when it comes to environmental issues of a local nature. In particular, women with children are the people who exhibit more concern about local environmental issues. There is no consensus about why this tendency exists. The finding that women with children often tend to exhibit more concern about local environmental issues really does not answer the question why. Could it simply be a case where women consciously see the immediate need to protect their children? If so, this would suggest that women's concern about the environment may also be instrumental.

Or is there some more fundamental factor influencing such patterns? There does not seem to be very clear evidence on this issue.

Is There Class-Based Bias in Attitudes Toward the Environment? It has been suggested that those who are most supportive of government intervention on behalf of the environment are disproportionately wealthy and from upper-middle or upper-class backgrounds (Mohai, 1985). This is the way the "environmental movement" has been characterized by a number of people, including the national Republican Study Committee (most Republican members of the U.S. House of Representatives), and some leading journalists and scholars. This argument stems from the idea that there may well be a trade-off between jobs and the environment, and that people who are well-off would be the least threatened by any loss of jobs that might result from rigorous environmental regulation. On the other hand, working-class people, who may be employed in industries most financially hurt by environmental regulation, feel directly threatened by the potential loss of jobs, and consequently feel less urgency to protect the environment.

Although there is not an abundance of information about the extent to which a class bias exists in attitudes toward the environment, it would appear that working-class people are just as concerned about environmental issues as are those who are economically well-off. For example, analysis of survey research results by Ladd (1982, p. 19) revealed only small differences among people from four different income levels. In other words, people whose incomes are relatively low are not more likely to oppose efforts at environmental protection.

A Summary of the Context of Environmental Policy-Making in America

In an effort to build a picture of the basic context in which environmental policies are made in the United States, this chapter reviewed some of the more salient environmental problems of our time. This review revealed that there is reason to believe the nation and the world face a number of significant threats to the quality of the physical environment, including threats to air associated with acid rain, global warming or the greenhouse effect, depletion of the ozone layer of the earth's atmosphere, and radon gas exposure; and threats to water from acid rain itself, the disposal of hazardous wastes, accidental spills of oil and chemicals, overuse of chemical fertilizers and pesticides, and inadequate sewage treatment. These do not constitute all of the major environmental threats faced today. Problems such as asbestos in buildings, lead from paint and other sources, radon gas exposure, exportation of hazardous products, use of genetically engineered organisms in industry, and exposure to health risks in the workplace are all very important, challenging, and even controversial environmental issues. Yet space constraints prevent a thorough investigation of all of these.

There was also an introduction to some of the debate concerning the social and political values that underlie so much of the environmental protection discussion. This introduction revealed that there are a number of different clashes of values that help in developing an understanding of how people can often come to very different conclusions about environmental protection.

Additionally, a picture of public opinion toward the environment and environmental protection was built, showing how the public's attitudes seem to have changed over time. This discussion also raised the possibility that some of the common wisdom about the public's attitudes may not be correct. Clearly there is substantial support for environmental protection, and this support persists even when people are faced with the prospect of trade-offs. Most people, however, are of the firm opinion that the environment can and should be protected without serious detriment to the economy.

It was also found that there is not very much difference between men and women when it comes to attitudes toward national-level environmental issues, nor is there much difference between higher- and lower-income people. Indeed, support for environmental protection is relatively high among nearly all groups of people in America. Women do, however, reveal somewhat more concern about local environmental issues, such as the potential environmental impact of local industrial facilities.

With discussions of these basic environmental problems, the value bases for many environmental disputes and controversies, and public opinion concerning environmental protection, out of the way, it is almost time to start looking at some additional salient controversies surrounding specific environmental policies. Before doing this, however, a general outline of the policy-making processes in the United States can help in understanding elements of controversies in public environmental politics. So it is this issue, the policy-making process, that is the subject of Chapter 2.

2

The Role of Government in the Environment
The Policy-Making Processes

Before investigating actual environmental policies and associated controversies, it is necessary to examine some background to the making of public policies in the United States. This chapter begins by providing a general framework of public policy-making. The analysis of policy-making is less interested in the *results* of public policies and more interested in the *processes* through which attempts are made to achieve these results. After presenting many examples of how this policy-making process framework is applied to environmental decisions, the chapter concludes with a focused examination of the process through which federal environmental regulations are established.

A General Outline of the Policy-Making Processes in the United States

When people speak of the policy-making process, they are usually referring to a series of steps or stages that various political actors go

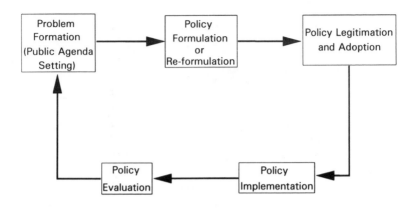

Figure 2.1. The Public Policy-Making Process

through in the making of governmental decisions. The policy-making process has been described in many different ways, with different and sometimes widely varied terminology, and with many different substantive applications. Nevertheless, the policy-making process is usually described as constituting a "cycle" having about five or six major interrelated steps or stages. As depicted in Figure 2.1, the policy-making process is usually described as being composed of *problem formation, policy formulation, policy legitimation, policy adoption, policy implementation,* and *policy evaluation.* Sometimes the policy legitimation stage is considered part of the policy adoption stage.

The problem formation stage of the policy-making process consists of all of the events and actions that take place to elevate some issue onto the public agenda. At any given time, there are many issues that are clearly not on the public agenda—they are issues not generally considered to be important enough to warrant serious public policy responses. But some issues do go through a process of being transformed into public issues, which are perceived as serious enough to deserve governmental attention. The process that characterizes such issues is referred to as the *problem formation* or agenda-setting stage of the policy-making process.

Once an issue is considered to be important and serious enough to warrant governmental action, this usually stimulates numerous proposals about the best way to deal with the problem. The process involving the development of these proposals is most often referred to as the *policy formulation* stage. It is here that alternative ways of addressing the problem are formulated and put forth as viable solutions. As described later, this policy formulation stage often involves a variety of actors and political interests.

The *policy legitimation* stage of the policy-making process encompasses all of the efforts to mobilize political support on behalf of one or another of the proposals to address the problem. When interest groups, industries, elected officials, or others work to develop support for a specific set of proposals to address an environmental problem, they are engaged in trying to legitimate that set of proposals. In actuality, policy legitimation activities take place throughout the policy-making process, very frequently occurring during policy formulation, during implementation, and so on.

After alternative proposals to address the issue have been formulated, and political support for one or more of them has been mobilized, one of these proposals, or some combination of proposals, may be selected as the official governmental response or policy. This formal selection from among the various alternatives is usually referred to as the *policy adoption* stage. In federal policy, this stage most frequently involves actions of Congress in passing legislation. In the states, it involves enactment of laws by state legislatures. As noted later, policies can actually be adopted by agencies other than Congress or state legislatures, such as the courts, or the president or governor by executive order.

Perhaps the most important stage in environmental policy-making processes is *policy implementation,* which refers to what happens to policy adoptions, laws, or decisions after they are passed by Congress, a state legislature, or another decision maker. The greatest portion of the implementation stage involves administrative agencies. Almost all legislation, once passed by a legislature, requires some other agency to put it into effect. A number of agencies play critical roles in the implementation of federal environmental policy. Of course, the federal Environmental Protection Agency (EPA) is the agency with the greatest responsibility for implementing federal environmental policies. Although implementation consists of many different kinds of agency activities, most implementation efforts focus on either the writing and issuing of regulations themselves, or the enforcement of those regulations or elements of specific legislation. The federal agencies most frequently engaged in implementing environmental policy will be examined shortly.

Finally, policies that are implemented need to be assessed as to whether they work, whether they produce the intended results, the extent to which they may produce unintended consequences, and so on. This stage of the policy-making process is referred to as *policy evaluation*. Policy evaluation is frequently designed to provide feedback into the policy-making process, presumably stimulating policy reformulation, revision, or, in rare cases, termination. In other words, once a policy has been in effect, evaluation can provide information about how it needs to be changed to make it more effective. Evaluation sometimes plays an important role when legislation is scheduled for renewal. Rather than simply extending an existing law, Congress, for example, might take this opportunity to redesign new legislation, at least partly in response to evaluations of earlier legislation.

It is important to recognize that these stages constitute a framework within which the policy-making process can be viewed or investigated. What occurs in these stages for one piece of legislation or policy area might be quite different from what occurs for another piece of legislation. Even legislation dealing with the same basic issues but at different points in time, such as air pollution or water pollution, can experience very different policy-making processes. While there may be identifiable stages in each process, the details of what happens are often quite different. Many examples of this will be presented in later chapters.

The Environmental Problem Formation Stage: Public Agenda Setting

Before the 1960s it was rare for anyone to speak of either the environment or environmental policy. But starting in the 1960s and continuing through the 1970s and 1980s and into the 1990s, the environment has been seen increasingly as an important issue, even a problem, by the American people. As noted in Chapter 1, by the early 1970s the environment, as a general concern, was clearly on the public agenda. Although there is not an abundance of information about the detailed processes associated with public agenda setting, at least one observer has tried to elaborate five major steps that are comprised in the agenda setting process, or what he calls the ecology "issue-attention cycle."

Downs (1972) describes these steps as applied to environmental issues. The first step is what he calls the "pre-problem" period, that period of time when public attention is generally lacking. The next step, called "alarmed discovery and euphoric enthusiasm," results from some dramatic event or series of events. This is when public awareness becomes heightened, and the initial demands are placed on government to "do something." Thus, as people heard news reports of the Exxon *Valdez* oil spill off the coast of Alaska, there arose public alarm and outrage. The third step—"realizing the costs of significant progress"—begins a period in which people start to recognize how expensive or difficult the environmental problem would be to correct. This is followed by an apparently imperceptible transformation into the fourth step, a period in which public enthusiasm gradually begins to die down. Here, it becomes evident to many that some type of sacrifice would be necessary to pursue environmental improvement. Depending on what kind of sacrifice the public might face, enthusiasm may well begin to abate. Finally, the fifth step, the "post-problem" period, occurs after public interest has declined. This could result in initiation of public policy or program efforts (i.e., it could lead into the policy formulation stage of the policy-making process), or interest could simply decline until another set of events starts the process anew.

It is not clear that this issue-attention cycle accurately characterizes all effort at environmental policy-making. It is also not clear whether, or to what extent, environmental problems must experience such an attention cycle in order to reach subsequent policy-making stages. For example, many environmental problems reach the public agenda without specific or dramatic events. Significant progress has been made in pursuing public policies toward acid rain even though there does not seem to have been any clear set of specific events that preceded legislative action. Rather, the problems of acid rain have persisted over a fairly long period of time, and the damage caused by acid rain occurs gradually over time. Nonetheless, there are many environmental issues that do reach the public agenda after experiencing elements of the issue-attention cycle.

One of the early events that moved issues of the environment onto the public agenda was information about the use and abuse of the pesticide DDT. In 1964 Rachel Carson wrote *Silent Spring,* a book that described the apparent fact that DDT use in agriculture was causing the demise of various bird populations. The title *Silent Spring* implied that unless something was done about DDT, there might be no birds left to sing in the spring. After much debate, the release of a major independent commission report, and considerable interagency disagreement, the Nixon administration finally announced, in 1969, a 2-year phaseout of agricultural uses of DDT (Bosso, 1987, p. 140).

A number of other major events contributed to increasing public concern about the environment through the 1960s. Reports of serious air pollution in Pittsburgh and other major cities, major oil spills off the coast of California, seriously contaminated waterways, such as Lake Michigan and the Cuyahoga River in Cleveland, and other events contributed to a general sense that our physical environment was somehow in trouble. Events through the 1970s ensured that public concern about the environment would continue. Reports of chemical contamination at the Love Canal area of New York State, the nuclear power plant accident at Three Mile Island in Pennsylvania, and other major events helped to cement environmental concern.

Many specific issues currently thought of as serious or impending environmental problems have not always been on the public agenda. For example, it was not until perhaps the early to mid-1980s that the issue of global warming made its way onto the public agenda. Many people had been discussing and writing about the possible greenhouse effect, but few people paid much attention. Hazardous waste was not generally seen as a problem until perhaps the late 1970s. And issues such as radon gas and genetic engineering did not make their way onto the public agenda until fairly recently.

Environmental agenda setting is heavily influenced by developments in science and technology. This occurs for two reasons. First, science and technology are responsible for creating many environmental problems as by-products of other activities. For example, the development of modern air-conditioning played a key role in stimulating the manufacture and use of freon, a chlorofluorocarbon gas that has been identified as a possible cause of the thinning of the ozone layer. Second, science and technology provide new and clearer understanding of the causes, and sometimes the consequences, of environmental problems. It was not until scientists discovered a possible link between pollution and global warming that the greenhouse effect started to make its way onto the public agenda; when scientists discovered the link between radon gas exposure and health consequences, radon gas became a matter for the public agenda. So science and technology often play a significant role in defining the environmental policy agenda.

Changes in scientific or technical knowledge, however, may not be enough to place a specific environmental issue on the public agenda. Frequently, some form of citizen or interest group action must accompany changes in information. Not uncommonly, there are major economic interests in American society that do not want to see a specific issue placed on the public agenda—either because of the obvious economic threat to that industry, because the industry does not believe the new scientific evidence to be credible or conclusive, or both. In extreme cases, an industry may even take efforts to suppress information about the harmful effects of a polluting agent. For example, there is some evidence that the asbestos industry suppressed for many years knowledge about the harmful effects of asbestos exposure (Brodeur, 1985, pp. 97-131). This illustrates the clashes between underlying values of economics versus humanism, and between science and economics versus practical politics, described in Chapter 1. The point is that there may be political interests willing and able to prevent an issue from becoming part of the public agenda, even in the face of technical or scientific knowledge. In these cases, unless some other political catalyst, such as a public interest or citizens' group, counteracts this industry influence, an issue may never make it onto the public agenda.

The Policy Formulation Stage

Once a problem has been identified and recognized as potentially worthy of public policy response, activities often turn to the policy formulation process. The principal activities of this process revolve around defining various alternative ways that the earlier identified problem can be addressed. In the policy formulation process, these alternatives usually refer specifically to alternative legislation or statutes that could be enacted by the legislature. Very often there is not a single best way or a consensus about trying to rectify an environmental problem, so a number of different legislative proposals may be put forth as plausible ways of effecting environmental improvement.

Alternative environmental policy formulations in the form of proposed legislation emerge from many different sources. Interest groups are frequently engaged in developing and offering specific solutions to problems. This might include major corporations, or industry or trade associations, with a clear stake in the problem. For example, the automobile industry has been very active in proposing legislation to deal with air pollution. Of course, sometimes such major actors may simply choose to oppose someone else's efforts, and these actions are usually thought of as being part of the policy legitimation process. There are other kinds of interest groups—sometimes referred to as public interest groups—such as the Conservation Law Foundation, the Sierra Club, the Environmental Defense Fund, and many others, which frequently offer legislative proposals as alternative ways of redressing environmental problems.

Regardless of whether alternative proposals originate from interest groups, many of the alternative proposals are put forth by government itself. Usually such proposals are produced by one or another government agency, often the agency that would ultimately have responsibility for enforcing or implementing any environmental law that is enacted. In federal policy-making, the EPA is a frequent formulator of policy alternatives. There are other federal agencies or actors, such as the Occupational Safety and Health Administration (OSHA), the Department of Health and Human Services, and the Surgeon General, to name a few, that have been involved in formulating policy proposals in the form of legislation. In issues involving state laws, state environmental protection agencies are often key actors in formulating proposals for environmental protection legislation.

Environmental Policy Legitimation and Adoption

After legislative proposals have emerged, policy-making turns on the process of legitimating one of these. This process consists of the actions taken by any party to line up support for, or opposition to, any given legislative proposal. In this process, various actors may try to mobilize and stimulate support for one piece of legislation. Not uncommonly, interest groups will mobilize opposition to legislative proposals that they consider harmful to their interests. Legitimation also involves activities to formulate political strategies to make one alternative sound much better than others.

Legitimation activities feed directly into the process of adopting environmental policy. Environmental policy adoption processes involve the actions of members of legislatures leading up to and including voting for or against enactment. This process is usually started with the formal introduction of a bill in Congress or a state legislature. It may include the activities associated with legislative committee hearings, the process actually used by the legislature to dispose of the legislation, and even the interpersonal politicking—bargaining, logrolling, and the like—surrounding a legislative proposal.

A couple of short examples might help to illustrate the kinds of activities these processes sometimes involve. In 1969 Congress enacted the National Environmental Policy Act (NEPA), really the first major piece of legislation addressing a wide range of environmental problems.

Perhaps the most significant accomplishments of NEPA were the creation of EPA's forerunner, the Council on Environmental Quality (CEQ), the requirement that all federal agencies prepare environmental impact statements analyzing the ecological effects of agencies' decisions, and the creation of opportunities for extensive judicial review of NEPA's implementation.

According to Liroff (1976, pp. 10-35), a number of factors combined to explain why Congress enacted this legislation. First, there were several influential members of Congress who, despite having some differences in philosophy about environmental protection and some apparent jurisdictional disagreements, generally believed that major federal legislation was needed. Henry Jackson (D-Washington) and Edmund Muskie (D-Maine) apparently took part in intense negotiations to produce this legislation. Second, perhaps because of the rather vague language in the bill itself, potentially affected industry groups apparently paid little attention to NEPA until after it became law. And third, there was rising concern among the general public that something should be done to check environmental degradation. These factors helped to create a specific set of congressional processes leading to NEPA's passage.

Another example of the policy legitimation and adoption process comes from the enactment of the Clean Air Act Amendments of 1970, discussed more fully in Chapter 3. This legislation is a totally new approach to improving the quality of the air. Studies by Charles O. Jones (1974, 1975) provide cogent descriptions of the processes through which this legislation achieved redefinition. He suggests that the more typical bargaining and negotiation that take place between advocates of controlling pollution and affected regulated interests, especially polluting industries and the automobile manufacturing industry, were essentially absent in 1970. The main reason why industries were relatively silent on the Clean Air Act Amendments of 1970 is that, under the Clean Air Amendments of 1967, each state was required to set its own standards for limits on air pollution emissions. Any industry opposition to the 1970 Amendments was apparently tempered because having a single national air quality standard was seen by industry as cheaper and better than having to comply with 50 different standards.

By comparing the politics of policy-making across many specific environmental decisions, it is possible to identify some persistent general, albeit certainly not universal, patterns. Although there are numerous exceptions, environmental policy adoption processes tend to be associated with relatively unstable political relationships among actors

(Congress and congressional committees, interest groups, and agency officials), with the relative strength of given actors changing rapidly over time. Members of Congress involved in one set of environmental legislation are likely to be somewhat different from those involved in another set of legislation. Interest groups active and influential in one set of issues might be less active or influential in subsequent issues. Policy adoption process also tends to be characterized by considerable amounts of bargaining and compromise, and by a variety of political interests or actors sharing or competing for political influence (Ripley & Franklin, 1980, p. 22).

Environmental Policy Implementation and Enforcement

After legislative adoption of an environmental law, it is turned over to an administrative agency for implementation and/or enforcement. The implementation process consists of all of the actions taken by this administrative agency and by other actors in an effort to put this law into effect. Sometimes the implementation process consists of an administrative agency simply setting up administrative procedures to monitor activities. Sometimes it consists of simply collecting information. Frequently, environmental policy implementation requires an agency, often the EPA, to formulate and put into effect regulations that have the effect of law (Durant, 1984). In other words, the EPA is often given the responsibility for deciding, through issuing regulations, what the specific environmental law will be. So when the EPA issues standards specifying that the air cannot contain more than 10 milligrams of carbon monoxide per cubic meter of air in any given 8-hour period, as it did in 1971, this is a partial result of a sometimes lengthy process of promulgating air pollution regulations (Rosenbaum, 1977, p. 134).

In creating such regulations, the administrative agency may go through a process that resembles a full-scale policy-making process (Doniger, 1978). Alternative proposals are often put forth as proper ways to regulate or improve the environment. Such alternative proposals can originate with the agency, or as suggested previously, can be made by various interest groups. For example, when Congress passed the Federal Environmental Pesticides Control Act (FEPCA) of 1972 to allow the regulation of pesticides used by farmers, agricultural interest groups suggested to the EPA what form those regulations should take (Bosso, 1987, pp. 181-186). The EPA and OSHA, and their environmental regulatory processes, will be described in much more detail below.

Although the federal EPA is the agency charged with implementing most national environmental legislation, not all environmentally relevant implementation falls to the EPA. The regulation of pesticides, insecticides, and fertilizers in agriculture often falls to the domain of the U.S. Department of Agriculture and to the Food and Drug Administration (FDA). Regulation of environmental hazards in the workplace typically falls to the Occupational Safety and Health Administration (OSHA) in the U.S. Department of Labor, and the National Institute for Occupational Safety and Health (NIOSH), a part of the Centers for Disease Control. Analysis of health effects from environmental contamination is partly the responsibility of the U.S. Public Health Service, including its National Institutes of Health. Responsibility for protecting many waterways falls to the U.S. Army Corps of Engineers. Regulation of nuclear power plants, and the nuclear wastes they produce, is the responsibility of the federal Nuclear Regulatory Commission. Frequently, environmental policy must be implemented by more than one agency at the same time. However, the EPA is the agency given primary responsibility for what is usually thought of as environmental policy implementation.

Another major part of environmental policy implementation consists of the enforcement function (Russell, Harrington, & Vaugh, 1986). Enforcement simply consists of an agency making efforts and taking actions to ensure that the targets of rules and regulations (i.e., polluting parties) comply with these regulations. While the regulations issued by federal agencies carry the weight of law, there is nothing to guarantee that all affected parties will automatically comply. Thus, there is a clear need for the agency to engage in efforts to ensure that the regulations are followed. This enforcement function may take many forms. It sometimes involves having the agency monitor or inspect the targets of regulation to determine whether compliance is taking place.

In cases where compliance is not taking place, the agency must then decide how to obtain compliance. Sometimes the agency will simply call attention to the noncompliance with the hope that the polluting party will voluntarily correct the problem. At other times, the agency will negotiate with the polluting party to come to some agreement about how compliance will be achieved. Occasionally, when failure to comply has caused some environmental damage or has incurred the cost of rectifying environmental damage, the agency will try to recover the costs as part of the negotiations. In severe instances, usually where a polluting party has established a clear pattern of noncompliance over time, the agency might recommend to the Justice Department that legal action be taken against the polluter. Depending on the legislation under which such action is taken, the agency might recommend action against polluters in civil courts or, in a few instances, in criminal court (Hawkins, 1984).

Almost from the time of the first federal involvement in environmental policy, some responsibility for implementing national environmental policy has been either delegated or relegated to the states. Nearly every state has its own version of the EPA, a single agency given primary responsibility for state environmental regulation implementation. Frequently, the EPA works with its state counterparts in an effort to find workable ways of putting national policies into effect. This federal/state interaction is discussed later when we address the issue of environmental policy-making in the federal system.

Regardless of which agencies are involved with implementation, there are some general patterns to their processes. For the most part, implementation patterns or experiences differ from policy to policy, and may even differ within a policy area over time (O'Brien, Clarke, & Kamieniecki, 1984). So the nature of implementation associated with the 1977 Clean Air Act Amendments was quite different from that of the 1977 Clean Water Act, or even the 1990 Clean Air Act. Yet Ripley and Franklin (1980, 1982) suggest that implementation of environmental policies, examples of what they refer to as "protective regulatory policies," or policies explicitly designed to protect people from undesirable effects of private sector activities, is inherently politically volatile. The implementation process tends to be highly visible to a variety of potentially opposed interests, including those that are the targets of any regulatory restrictions, and environmental groups that might see themselves as guardians of the environment. Additionally, congressional oversight of the implementation process is rather sporadic, focusing more on complaints and crises than on day-to-day operations (Ripley & Franklin, 1982, p. 155).

There is a natural tension built into the implementation process since a government agency is given responsibility for trying to alter behavior of other organizations. Because this behavior is usually motivated by the pursuit of private economic benefits, the government agency is generally perceived as an impediment to achieving those benefits. This, of course, possesses characteristics of several value clashes, as described in Chapter 1, especially the clash between economic efficiency and humanism. The political consequence is that the regulated industry places increasing pressure on the regulatory agency to do a less-vigorous job of regulation than might otherwise be the case (Ripley & Franklin, 1982, pp. 152-155). This might become manifest in an agency's choosing to exercise little in the way of enforcement authority; sometimes it results in an agency's changing an existing regulation to be more favorable to the regulated industry. This type of pressure, as will be discussed in later chapters, helps explain why the EPA has issued regulations or standards on clean air and clean water, only to later revise these standards downward or to make exceptions for specific polluters.

Environmental policy implementation is all the more volatile because of fairly strong and well-organized nonindustry advocacy groups. These groups function as watchdogs, monitoring the agencies' activities, and often lobby the agencies or members of Congress when agency actions appear to undermine the goal of producing a cleaner environment (Meier, 1985, pp. 139-174). Thus, even if industry pressure on the agency is strong, there is some degree of countervailing pressure to dissuade the agency from being responsive only to the regulated industry. The volatility associated with the environmental policy implementation process is evidenced by frequently shifting alliances on the part of the implementors, sometimes siding with advocates of vigorous regulation and sometimes siding with advocates of less regulation.

The main consequence of this set of relationships is that routine implementation is difficult to establish. As soon as EPA begins to establish a routine way of implementing a given program or policy, there are immediate pressures to alter that routine. This is especially true if there is a change in presidential administration or high-level federal personnel. For example, when EPA administrator William Ruckelshaus resigned and was replaced by Lee Thomas in 1985, this apparently opened up many issues related to EPA's developing air pollution "bubble policy" that had previously seemed resolved (Liroff, 1986, pp. 59-60).

Environmental Policy Evaluation and Reformulation

After implementation gets under way, much legislation and many programs carry with them requirements that they be evaluated. This evaluation stage focuses on the activities of various actors who are engaged in evaluating the program's effectiveness or other consequences. Usually evaluation is designed to try to determine whether and to what extent the program worked. It might also investigate the reasons why the program did not work as intended. And frequently evaluations examine what, if anything, could be done to make the program more effective. This latter type of question is designed to influence the reformulation of new policy. In other words, evaluation results are often used as the basis for proposing modification or alternatives to existing legislation. So evaluation can become a mechanism for feedback into the process. When this occurs, the process essentially starts anew, resulting in some type of change in the law and in changed implementation.

After the federal government launched its 1970 Clean Air programs, efforts were made to evaluate whether these programs had the desired effects—was the nation's air cleaner, were automobiles emitting less pollution than before, and so on. Typically, evaluations attempt to establish whether the policy or program caused the desired effect, or whether the program caused some undesirable consequence. When White (1982) evaluated the effort to reduce automobile emissions, research was aimed at determining whether the federal regulations had the desired effect, or whether improvements in air quality could be attributed to factors other than the regulations themselves. This is an example of fairly typical policy evaluation. Subsequent chapters present many examples of the role of evaluation in policy reformulation.

With this basic description of the overall environmental policy-making process in mind, attention can now be focused on providing some greater detail of what happens in the policy implementation and enforcement stage. This description focuses on what is frequently involved in federal administration of environmental policy, including the process through which many federal agencies write the rules that constitute formal environmental regulations. These processes themselves become the subject of some controversy.

Federal Environmental Policy Implementation, Enforcement, and Regulation: The Regulatory Activities of EPA and OSHA

Earlier, the environmental implementation process was presented in general outline and some examples of the general patterns of this process as experienced by federal agencies were also provided. Because this process, especially the process through which federal environmental regulations are established, plays such a dominant role in federal environmental policy, it is worthwhile to spend a little more time explaining what this process looks like. As a result, the reader will develop a clearer idea of how formidable a task EPA and other environmental agencies have in trying to implement legislation.

The Federal Environmental Protection Agency (EPA)

As noted earlier, the federal environmental policy implementation process focuses on actions of administrative and regulatory agencies given authority by Congress. In contemporary America, most of this authority has been given to the EPA, which President Bush proposed to elevate to the level of a cabinet department. Before the general process through which the EPA formulates and implements environmental regulations is explained, a brief review of this agency's history is in order.

The federal EPA was created in 1970 by executive order of President Richard Nixon. This order established the EPA as an independent agency that reports directly to the president. With this reorganization, Nixon accomplished what some advocates of environmental regulation had failed to do for the better part of the 1960s. Nixon's apparent intent was both to create an agency that provided him with centralized political control and to preempt congressional action to create environmental agencies. However, the effect was to consolidate into a single agency environmental regulatory functions previously performed in many different federal agencies (Rosenbaum, 1977, pp. 122-125). From the time of its inception, the EPA's responsibilities have grown as Congress has given it more and more legislation on which to base its actions. From 1970 to 1980 the EPA grew to become the largest federal regulatory agency (CQWR, 1981, p. 4). EPA has a central office in Washington, D.C., and 10 regional offices covering the entire country. The regional offices frequently work with state environmental agencies to implement or seek compliance with federal standards.

The relatively short history of the EPA may be characterized in three major eras. In the first era, from its inception until about 1981, the EPA took seriously the tasks of protecting and improving the environment. During this period, EPA was given responsibility for implementing numerous pieces of legislation, and consequently the agency's budget and employment rolls increased accordingly. The agency made efforts, through its staff of lawyers, to not only legally enforce but also gain through voluntary action compliance with environmental laws. It also began developing an unusually strong internal scientific capacity by establishing its own research division and hiring many competent scientists.

Soon after the EPA's creation, Congress enacted a number of pieces of legislation giving the EPA responsibility and authority for environmental protection implementation. This legislation includes the watershed National Environmental Policy Act of 1970 (NEPA), the Clean Air Act Amendments of 1970, the Water Quality Improvement Act of 1970, the Resource Recovery Act of 1970, the 1972 Amendments to the Federal Water Pollution Control Act, and subsequent legislation. Each piece of legislation gave the EPA responsibility for affecting environmental policy in a specific area, and sometimes required the EPA to fill in the gaps in statutory language or intent. For example, in the 1972 Water Pollution Control Amendments, Congress stated that the EPA should ensure that by 1977 private industry must use the "best practicable technology," and by 1983 it should ensure the use of the "best available technology," to end water pollution practices. It then fell to the EPA to determine, and subsequently enforce, what these technologies were. In 1970, when Congress created OSHA, the agency was required to "set the standard which most adequately assures . . . on the basis of the best available evidence, that no employee will suffer material impairment of health or functional capacity" from exposure to environmental pollutants on the job. It then became the task of OSHA to define and enforce standards regarding adequate assurance, material impairment, and many other terms conveyed in the enabling legislation (Bryner, 1987, p. 122).

While it may seem somewhat irresponsible for Congress to leave such important issues to a bunch of bureaucrats, Congress did this for two central reasons. First, Congress could not possibly know in 1970 what the "best available evidence" or in 1972 what the "best technologies" would be 5 or 10 years down the road. And second, the more specific the language of legislation, the more difficult it often is to come to agreement and pass that legislation. However, as is often the case with environmental legislation, this placed an immense amount of decision-making, responsibility, and discretion directly into the hands of the regulatory agencies. In effect, agencies are given responsibility for filling in the gaps—providing the details not expressed in the legislation itself. Later, other examples of the exercise of this discretion will be presented, and it will be argued that this often becomes the place where political controversy arises.

The second era, from 1981 through 1983, saw the EPA retrench from its environmental protection charge. In 1981 the newly elected President Reagan appointed Anne Gorsuch (later using her married name,

Anne Gorsuch Burford) to be administrator of the EPA. As part of Reagan's emphasis on deregulation, Gorsuch proceeded to fundamentally change the goals and actions of the EPA. From 1981 to 1983, the operating budget of the EPA was slashed by some 29% (not including grants for local sewer construction); the number of full-time employees was reduced by nearly 3,000; and many important positions were either left unfilled or filled by temporary appointments (Meier, 1985, pp. 164-165). Gorsuch and Rita Lavelle, the EPA's director of the Superfund program charged with cleaning up hazardous waste sites, apparently embarked on a program of delaying environmental regulation and clean-up, making decisions that worked to the benefit of specific polluting corporations, and lying to Congress about what they were doing (Meier, pp. 163-165). Congressional investigations turned up cases where hazardous waste clean-up decisions were made for purely political purposes, and enforcement of environmental laws was selective at best. Subsequently, Lavelle was convicted of lying to Congress, and received a prison sentence.

The third era, from about 1983 to the present, saw the gradual reinstatement of concern about environmental protection, this time with explicit efforts to balance environmental protection against its economic costs. This reinstatement started when William Ruckelshaus, the agency's first administrator, was reappointed as head of the agency. Ruckelshaus (1983-1985) and his successors, Reagan appointee Lee Thomas (1985-1989) and Bush appointee William Reilly, have oriented the agency toward fulfilling the intent of the legislation it is responsible for implementing while also using its legal discretion to achieve a balance of economic and environmental interests.

Shortly after taking office, President Bush proposed to elevate the EPA to cabinet-level status. This newly proposed Department of Environmental Affairs would possess all the same responsibilities and would be governed by the same enabling legislation as the EPA. Indeed, it is not clear what, if anything, would change through this elevation. Perhaps because President Bush took office with high expectations that his administration would be much more sympathetic to environmental concern than his predecessor's, the Bush administration may feel the need to take concrete action without necessarily putting greater burdens on the already overburdened federal budget. As with many federal reorganization proposals, the effort to elevate the EPA may have much greater political and symbolic importance than implications for the quality of the environment (Seidman & Gilmour, 1986).

The Occupational Safety and Health Administration (OSHA)

Another major regulatory actor in environmental policy making is the Occupational Safety and Health Administration (OSHA) and its several companion agencies. OSHA was created and placed within the U.S. Department of Labor in 1970 when Congress passed the Occupational Health and Safety Act. This Act also established the Occupational Safety and Health Review Commission, an independent commission that oversees and reviews OSHA enforcement decisions, and the National Institute for Occupational Safety and Health (NIOSH), a new research division of the National Institutes of Health.

OSHA's enabling charge called for it to ensure "so far as possible every working man and woman in the nation safe and healthful working conditions." This initial charge required OSHA to issue, within 2 years, regulations codifying any "national consensus standards" and practices already being used by industry. OSHA was also empowered to issue any regulations that would result in improved health and safety of American workers. According to Bryner, OSHA issued some 4,400 health and safety standards within the first month of its existence.

The EPA, OSHA, and Their Regulatory Functions

As already noted, when Congress enacts environmental legislation, it often gives the EPA or OSHA specific legal authority and responsibility for issuing environmental regulations that have the effect of law. In the earlier history of the EPA and OSHA, these regulations included setting specific standards to achieve legislatively specified goals, decisions about how and when to take actions against violators, and decisions about monitoring the progress toward achieving goals (Gaines, 1977; National Academy of Sciences, 1977). In more recent times, Congress has sometimes retained the responsibility for setting many standards, preferring to specify these in their statutes rather than delegating them to the EPA or OSHA. Since 1981 decisions about whether to issue regulations and the content of regulations have been centrally reviewed by the federal Office of Management and Budget (OMB), the major budget and management agency of the Executive Office of the President. Setting environmental standards is still very much a function performed by the EPA and by OSHA; however, whatever rule-making decisions that have to be made by EPA or OSHA use a similar regulatory decision-making process.

The Regulatory Decision-Making Process in a Nutshell

As with many federal regulatory agencies, the EPA and other environmental agencies exercise much of their authority by writing and issuing regulations or rules. *Rule making* is the administrative process that is intended to result in establishing regulations. The resulting regulations have the effect of law because they are authorized by congressional statutes. The basic steps in the rule making process for nearly all federal agencies are set by a single piece of national legislation, the Administrative Procedures Act, initially enacted in 1946 and amended many times since. Within the constraints of this Act, regulatory agencies tend to develop their own variations of the rule-making process (Schmandt, 1985). Bryner (1987, pp. 98-105) describes the process at EPA as involving some four phases, with each phase consisting of numerous activities.

The process of issuing regulations might be said to constitute a policy-making process within the broader policy-making process. This regulatory decision-making usually begins when the EPA or another agency is given explicit direction in legislation, or when administrators believe there is a need for a general rule to govern some aspect of a program or implementation effort. This results in the establishment of specific rule-making objectives—what the agency is going to try to achieve in issuing the resulting regulations—which are submitted to the Office of Management and Budget (OMB) for review. This OMB review checks to make sure that the goals of the agency's regulations conform to the goals of the president and the White House. Of course, it is not uncommon for the goals of the president and White House to be at odds with objectives at Congress, so this sometimes becomes a point of political controversy.

Once approved by OMB, the agency gives public notice in the *Federal Register* of the intent to issue regulations. This publication comes out daily and contains proposed or final regulations from all federal departments and agencies. At this point, the agency starts in earnest to write the regulations. Agency officials examine a variety of alternative regulations and analyze the impact of each alternative. In environmental regulation, such analyses frequently include in-depth study of economic costs, benefits, risks, and effectiveness. In 1981 President Reagan issued an Executive Order, which required not only that major rules have to demonstrate that the benefits of any regulation exceed the costs of the regulation, but also that the least costly alternative regulation was selected. Even though this Executive Order applies to all regulatory agencies, scientific, technical, and economic considerations are perhaps more important in formulating environmental regulations than in any other regulatory field simply because federal environmental regulation potentially affects such a wide range of private and public sector activities.

Once sufficient information has been assembled, agency officials put together draft regulations and circulate them to the most affected industries. Often the agency holds formal hearings to elicit reactions and information from industry representatives and outside experts. Based on what happens in these hearings, the agency may alter the regulations. Once the agency feels the regulations are adequate, it must publish them in the *Federal Register.* After these versions of the regulations are published, the public has the opportunity to respond by writing to the agency. Typically the written responses come from major interest groups that have both a stake in these regulations and the resources to follow developments in the *Federal Register.*

After a short time, agency officials evaluate these comments, along with congressional opinion, and decide whether and how to change the proposed regulations. Then the final regulations are written and submitted again to OMB, who reviews them and may approve them as written, ask for modifications, or block their issuance altogether. If OMB approves the regulations, they are published in the *Federal Register*. Only then do these regulations become law.

This entire process, from the time agency officials decide to issue regulations until the time the resulting regulations actually become law, can take a fairly long time, perhaps several years. According to Bryner, the rule-making process under current procedural guidelines at EPA takes a minimum of almost 3 years (1987, p. 99). While the short descriptions of the stages in the regulatory process are accurate depictions of environmental policy-making as far as they go, the actual process of issuing a specific regulation can be much more complicated. For example, a study of the EPA found that the actual number of steps in these processes can range anywhere from about 13 (as was the case in formulating the National Ambient Air Quality Standards under the Clean Air Act) to about 53 (Berry, 1984).

As long and complicated as this rule-making process may be, it might not end with the issuing of regulations. Frequently these final regulations are challenged and subjected to judicial review, where a party adversely affected by a regulation might sue the issuing agency to force the agency to modify or rescind the regulation (Rodgers, 1981). Thus the federal courts often play a significant role in determining the final content of environmental regulations (Leventhal, 1974).

The decade of the 1970s witnessed a marked growth in the use of the courts for the purpose of seeking environmental protection. Much of this growth is the result of the National Environmental Policy Act (NEPA), described earlier, although other federal and state legislation has also contributed to it. As noted earlier, NEPA required federal agencies to use environmental impact statements before embarking on major projects. The legislation also provided an opportunity for environmentalists to use the courts, through citizen lawsuit provisions, to force parties not complying with the legislation to do so. Very often, environmental interest groups would seize this opportunity to seek injunctions against environmentally damaging developments that had been unsuccessfully challenged through other means. Liroff (1976, p. 8) explains the involvement of the courts when he states that:

> Environmentalists' dissatisfaction with agency response, their desire to see an elaboration upon NEPA's broadly stated requirements, and their viewing NEPA as an ultimate weapon to use against on-going projects they hitherto had unsuccessfully opposed—all combined to push many vital decisions about NEPA's meaning into the courts.

Many other pieces of legislation have also contributed to the entry of the courts into the environmental regulatory process. Later chapters will make it clear that legislation intended to protect the environment has sometimes contained provisions for civil legal action to be taken either by government or by citizens against noncompliant parties. Some of the more recent legislation calls for specific criminal penalties against offending parties.

Melnick's (1983) study provides a prime example of the role of the courts in air pollution policy. This study examines the many ways and reasons why the courts have been used as an extension of the political system to provide access to policy decisions for a variety of groups and interests. Melnick argues that the involvement of the courts has had some unintended and often undesirable consequences. One example of the kind of impact the courts have had relates to judicial interpretation of the 1970 Clean Air Act Amendments. Here Melnick describes two major court cases that defined and even changed the goals of air pollution policy. In one of these cases, the court ruled that state implementation plans for air pollution control had to include provisions not just to ensure the attainment and maintenance of air quality standards, but also to prevent the deterioration of air that was already cleaner than the standards required. In another case, polluters were prohibited from achieving local ambient air standards by dispersing them over a wide area rather than by reducing actual emissions (Melnick, p. 71).

The involvement of the courts has been controversial for several reasons. One reason is that many people believe the courts had no clear statutory basis for making their decisions. This is an instance where some felt the courts were legislating air pollution policy rather than just providing an enforcement mechanism. In the example of the two cases that affected the clean air regulation, Congress apparently agreed with the courts since it enacted these provisions in the 1977 Clean Air Act Amendments (Melnick, p. 71).

As will be seen in later chapters, there are several other types of controversies over environmental regulations. Obviously controversies have erupted over the content of specific regulations, in situations where targeted industries are pitted against agency officials, and perhaps indirectly against Congress. Debate often takes place over the approach to regulation adopted by the relevant agency. For example, economists often argue that regulation should take place through creating market incentives, rather than through setting and enforcing specific standards. Sometimes controversies involve industries that are unintendedly affected by regulations. Frequently disagreements emerge over how and when agencies should take legal actions to enforce regulations against apparent violators. And since about 1980, controversy has emerged over the EPA's decisions either not to issue regulations authorized by Congress or to stretch out the process in an apparent delaying tactic. Such controversies frequently reflect real political differences, difference in opinion about what should be done to improve the environment, how it should be done, and who should pay the price. They also involve differences of opinion about the role of government in protecting the environment. The EPA and OSHA are not the only federal agencies involved in environmental regulation (Bryner, 1987, p. 184; Krimsky & Plough, 1988, pp. 13-74). But they are certainly the most active.

Risk Assessment in the Federal Regulatory Process

As noted in Chapter 1, controversy frequently involves a clash of values between science and humanism. There is perhaps no clearer manifestation of this clash than when risk assessment or risk analysis finds its way into the regulatory process. Risk assessment is a fairly technical and scientific endeavor, which tries to estimate the level of danger or hazard associated with exposure to specific environmental contaminants. Frequently, the EPA uses risk assessments to help guide decisions about allowable or permissible levels of pollution. Regulations issued by the EPA usually contain threshold levels of contaminants or pollutants. If pollution exceeds these thresholds, then some form of remedial or enforcement action might be triggered. Thus, it becomes important to briefly review both what risk assessment is and how it finds its way into the policy-making process.

According to the National Research Council, as practiced in the federal agencies, risk assessment consists of the efforts to characterize "the potential adverse health effects of human exposures to environmental hazards" (NRC, 1983, p. 18). Risk assessments typically take into consideration several elements: descriptions of the potential adverse health effects based on evaluation of epidemiological, clinical, toxicological, and other environmental research; extrapolation from these results to predict the type and extent of health effects in humans under given conditions of exposure; the number of persons exposed to a contaminant in varying amounts and for various lengths of time; and the nature of uncertainties inherent in the estimates of dangers. While most risk assessments are very technical, the National Research Council's definition also includes more qualitative assessments because "quantitative assessments of risk are not always feasible, and they may be eschewed by agencies for policy reasons" (NRC, 1983, p. 18).

Risk assessment is a process that usually results in quantitative estimates or predictions of how dangerous exposure to a given environmental pollutant is for humans (Leape, 1980). It is generally described as consisting of four major steps, although these steps can look very different, depending on the agency using them, the chemical or contaminant being analyzed, and the nature of scientific information available. In general outline, the first step consists of *identifying the hazard.* In this process, efforts are made to determine whether a given hazard can potentially cause specific health consequences. For example, can exposure to PCBs cause cancer? Can exposure to asbestos cause asbestosis? If the answer to this type of question is that there are no known health consequences, then the risk assessment process might go no further. In situations where available laboratory, clinical, toxicological, or other information suggests that there are known health effects, the risk assessment process includes a *dose-response assessment.*

The *dose-response assessment* is a process examining the relation between the size of the dose (or exposure) to a contaminant and the incidence of the health problem. Will exposure to even a tiny amount of asbestos cause asbestosis? Or is there some higher level of exposure that is necessary before asbestosis becomes a likely result? Such dose-response assessments also include probabilistic evaluations, which take into consideration the range of uncertainty associated with existing information. For example, what is the probability that people exposed to a given level of a contaminant will develop the specified health effect? Such dose-response assessments frequently try to take into consideration a variety of other factors, such as the intensity and length of exposure, the age of people likely to be exposed, and sometimes specific life-style factors. For example, are people exposed to a low level of airborne asbestos over a long period of time (say, 10 years) more likely to experience asbestosis than people exposed to much higher levels of asbestos over a short period of time (say, one day or a few hours)?

The next step in the risk assessment process is *exposure assessment,* consisting of an effort to estimate the actual intensity, frequency, and duration of human exposures to specific contaminants. It also investigates different ways that people can be exposed to the contaminant, and identifies specific groups of people who might be disproportionately likely to receive dangerous levels of exposure. For example, even though asbestos may be found to cause asbestosis at even very low doses (or levels of exposure), are people actually in danger of being exposed to asbestos? If so, are there particular people who are more likely to be exposed than others? Through what route does the asbestos enter into the environment in such a way as to produce this level of exposure? This exposure assessment often helps prescribe what kinds of regulatory actions might be warranted. For example, if asbestos exposure turns out to be most likely to occur in school children who attend schools with asbestos pipe insulation, then regulatory actions can be directed toward this particular form of exposure.

Finally, the risk assessment process includes *risk characterization.* This involves estimating the incidence of a health effect under various conditions. This is accomplished by combining the dose-response and exposure assessments. The final product usually is an estimate that a particular type of person is likely to experience a given level of exposure to a contaminant, and is at a particular risk of developing a specific health problem; or it could be an aggregate assessment, stating that given existing exposure levels of a contaminant, a certain number of people can be expected to develop a specific health problem over a specified period of time. For example, given existing levels of exposure of children to asbestos in the schools, 3 children out of every 100,000 would be expected to develop asbestosis by the age of 30.

As might be imagined, the risk assessment process is often very difficult, necessarily involving many judgments with less than full or perfect information (Raynor, 1984; Robins, Landrigan, Robins, & Fine, 1985). Many risk assessments are made with basic dose-response information derived from animal studies conducted in a laboratory. This information is sometimes used to make inferences about human dose-responses. Not everyone is convinced that such animal studies provide useful information about human dose-responses. As later chapters will show, parties who must comply with regulations aimed at reducing or eliminating exposure frequently point to the lack of direct human dose-response studies as reasons why they should not be regulated. For example, the risk assessment process might lead EPA to issue regulations requiring the banning of a specific chemical in industrial use. The industries that use this chemical might object because the information used to prepare the risk assessment, and ultimately the decision to ban the chemical, was derived from dose-responses in laboratory rats. To such parties, dose-response evidence from rodents is insufficient to justify imposing potential economic hardship on them.

Even though there may be many problems with the process of conducting risk assessments, risk assessments have come to play a major role in environmental regulation (Fiorino, 1990). Depending on the standards set in specific legislation, risk assessments might be used in determining what kind of required pollution abatement technology is specified in federal regulations, establishing allowable limits on the use of environmental agents, limiting the use of such agents, and in some cases, completely banning specific agents. Recently, some policy analysts and policymakers have noted that many decisions are made concerning specific environmental contaminants without regard for the relative risks posed by a wide range of environmental dangers. According to these criticisms, the federal government often expends considerable energy and resources trying to regulate one problem that in the overall picture is less hazardous than problems that receive little or no attention.

The apparent frustration that some analysts feel over this tendency for federal environmental policy to not always take risk assessments into consideration provides a prime illustration of the tension between science and humanism, and between science and practical politics. Advocates of relying on risk assessment typically feel that this scientific approach to rational decision-making is perhaps the only value-neutral way to decide on regulations and standards. However, in expressing frustration at the fact that federal environmental policies are frequently made without explicit reference to risk assessments, these critics imply that political considerations play a much greater role than they should in influencing policy decisions. On the other hand, critics of risk assessment frequently argue that risk assessments may appear to be scientific and value-neutral, but they are not. These critics often argue that risk assessments can be made to show whatever analysts want them to show, and that individual risk assessments are frequently used to justify decisions that are politically and/or economically beneficial to specific parties, at the expense of others. In this view, given scientific inability to establish indisputable risks, the only alternative way to make decisions is through some political process (Lindblom, 1980, pp. 18-25; Portney, 1991b).

Chief EPA administrators Lee Thomas (1985 to 1989) and his successor William Riley (appointed by President Bush in 1989) have argued that risk assessments should become explicit parts of broader policy-making decisions—decisions concerning where to place the EPA's finite resources to produce the greatest environmental improvement. In 1987 the EPA issued its first report *Unfinished Business,* the product of an internal evaluation comparing the relative risks posed by a wide range of environmental problems. Implicit in this report was the idea that some sort of shift in EPA priorities was necessary to maximize the agency's ability to improve the quality of the environment. In 1989 Chief Riley asked EPA's Science Advisory Board to review the earlier report and develop specific strategies for accomplishing its goals. The Science Advisory Board created a special committee, the Relative Risk Reduction Strategies Committee, to perform this task. When this committee issued its report in September 1990, it made a number of recommendations to EPA (USEPA, 1990). These recommendations, if followed, would probably have the effect of raising the level of importance of risk assessment in a full range of decisions about where EPA should be putting its resources, and for what kinds of activities EPA would request congressional funding.

Even though the use of risk assessment has increased and will probably continue to increase in importance in environmental policy-making, many people feel that the policy decisions cannot and should not be subordinated to technical studies, because such studies are likely to be based on less than perfect information. To critics of formal risk assessment, a more humanistic approach is necessary so that the EPA and other environmentally impacting agencies do not end up disguising value-laden decisions about which people are protected and which are not protected from environmental threats. As noted in Chapter 1, humanists frequently argue that some of the most important considerations—factors that should be taken into consideration—are not easily quantifiable. Indeed, they call into question the whole idea of quantitative risk assessment (Clarke, 1989; Hadden, 1984; Kunreuther & Ley, 1982). The use of formal risk assessments in the policy-making process becomes even more difficult and less well connected to actual policy decisions when there is a major difference between formally estimated risks and publicly perceived risks (House & Shull, 1985, pp. 138-140). For example, as long as people do not readily perceive that there are significant health risks from exposure to radon gas, it would be unlikely for the EPA to successfully regulate radon gas exposure.

Benefit-Cost Analysis in the Environmental Regulatory Process

Benefit-cost analysis has become an important element in environmental policy implementation because of two major events. First, as noted earlier, in 1981 President Reagan issued Executive Order 12291, which requires that all federal regulations be subjected to benefit-cost analysis before being issued. This Executive Order states, in part, that "Regulatory action shall not be undertaken unless the potential benefits to society from regulation outweigh the potential costs to society" (Biniek, 1986, p. 147; Smith, 1984). Thus, the EPA must demonstrate that the benefits of any proposed regulation outweigh the costs of that regulation. So if the EPA entertains issuing a regulation that would have the effect of improving the quality of air, it would have to show that the costs of complying with this regulation are not greater than the value of the benefits the regulation produces.

The second way that benefit-cost analysis has come to play a significant role in environmental regulation is through the enabling statutes enacted by Congress. Perhaps starting in the early 1980s, Congress increasingly added language to its environmental legislation, calling for that legislation to be implemented with careful consideration paid to the costs and benefits produced. In some cases, this language simply requires EPA or other agencies to set standards or regulations while taking into consideration costs of compliance, as was the case with the 1986 Safe Drinking Water Act Amendments. In later legislation, explicit language calls for agencies to assess and take into consideration the benefits and costs of all the aspects of environmental policy implementation.

The use of benefit-cost analysis may seem like a straightforward and perhaps commonsensical way to ensure that environmental regulation does not do more harm than good. Yet its use has not been without controversy, which stems from the fact that benefit-cost analysis is not infallible or value-neutral. Frequently, benefit-cost analysis is advocated as rigorous scientific methodology that will provide definitive answers as to the net value of environmental regulation (Peskin & Seskin, 1975). If one simply conducts a benefit-cost analysis on a given regulation, it can be shown clearly whether this regulation should become law, so the argument goes. However, benefit-cost analysis possesses particular problems and characteristics, which makes many people argue that it should not be a determining factor in whether regulations are issued (Biniek, 1986).

The central problem with benefit-cost analysis is that costs are much easier to quantify than are benefits. Stated in another way, the costs of a particular regulation can be documented fairly accurately, and dollar estimates of these costs provide a fairly accurate assessment of the costs that would be incurred. It is relatively easy to estimate how much it could cost for all coal-burning electric generating plants to install a particular technology to achieve cleaner air emissions. However, the benefits of any proposed regulation are much more difficult to accurately assess. There are many benefits that might accrue from a regulation that cannot easily be assessed, or at least cannot be assessed in a universally agreed upon way. If one of the benefits of cleaner air is that 1,000 people will live 10 years longer, how does one quantify and assign dollar values to this benefit? Experts in benefit-cost analysis have developed methods of assigning such dollar benefits (Zeckhauser, 1975), but needless to say, these estimates are not always readily accepted. Consequently, many people have questioned whether benefit-cost analysis can or should be used as the primary basis on which to make environment regulations (Baram, 1980; DeSanti, 1980; Swartzman, Liroff, & Croke, 1982).

Despite this, as already noted, benefit-cost analysis has indeed become a very important part of the environmental regulatory process. To critics of benefit-cost analysis, imposing its use on the regulatory process represents an attempt to guarantee that very beneficial regulations will never be issued. This is because the bias in benefit-cost analysis tends to be an underestimation of benefits and an accurate estimation of costs. So when actual benefits of any given regulation might be slightly greater than costs, the costs as revealed in benefit-cost analysis will almost always exceed the benefits. Thus, the use of what might seem a commonsensical way to ensure regulatory efficiency becomes a tool for introducing a conservative bias into the process, a bias that could well mask clashes of values over the role of government in society, in science versus humanism, and perhaps in others as well (Andrews, 1982, p. 117).

Environmental Policy-Making in the Federal System

The description of environmental policy-making, especially the decision processes of the EPA and OSHA, has focused on national or federal efforts. However, implementation of environmental policy takes place in the context of a national federal political system—one in which the federal government cannot, or might not always find it politically prudent to preempt state or local action. Federal legislation and EPA practice have evolved within the context of a particular set of intergovernmental relations. These relations can help define the role of government in environment protection.

The nature of the relationship between the EPA and the states varies according to the specific policy or environmental problem being addressed. Some legislation calls for very little interaction between federal and state agencies; other legislation suggests some degree of shared responsibility; and still other legislation simply calls for the EPA to provide technical and financial support for state and local programs. Lieber (1983) suggests that:

> In terms of the degree of national control and direction vis-à-vis state and local governments, [the Resource Conservation and Recovery Act of 1976] ranks in the middle between such basically national, almost preemptive, laws as the Toxic Substances Control Act and the Federal Insecticide, Rodenticide, and Fungicide Act on the one hand, and the EPA's noise, drinking water, and solid waste programs, which have

generally consisted of technical assistance and funding support to local and state programs.

The variation in relations between the EPA and state and local governments is something which has, in many policy areas, evolved over a period of time. In the earlier experiences with federal environmental legislation, Congress placed very little responsibility for environmental policy implementation with the federal government. For example, the Solid Waste Disposal Act of 1965 called for a modest federal role in seeking new and improved methods of safe and efficient solid waste disposal, while also calling for state and local governments to continue maintaining and operating disposal sites (Whitaker, 1976, p. 111). It was not until the Resource Recovery Act of 1970 that the federal government began to take on explicit authority and responsibility for solid and hazardous waste regulation. This tendency for an increasing federal role vis-à-vis state and local government apparently paralleled a shift in responsibilities for financing the construction of sewage facilities that took place through the 1960s. Indeed, despite the presence of an ideological bias in the White House and among some members of Congress opposing a strong federal role, most environmental policy now provides for substantial federal authority and responsibility. Examples of this are presented in subsequent chapters.

This variation in relations between the EPA and state and local governments has two related implications for environmental policy implementation. First, it means that the specific patterns of relationships (the patterns that characterize the policy implementation process) vary from policy area to area. Second, in some policy areas, most notably toxic and hazardous waste management, there is persistent tension and disagreement between the EPA and specific states. Frequently, the EPA desires to implement a program in one way, and a given state wants the EPA to implement it in another way. Sometimes states feel that the EPA is imposing requirements on them that prevent them from being responsive to their needs. Sometimes the states want the EPA to take financial and legal responsibility for program implementation. Often, federal legislation makes unclear the ways in which the states can act on their own to affect environmental problems. For example, the state of New Jersey imposed a "spill compensation" tax on industries to help finance hazardous waste cleanups. But the state was sued by a number of chemical and petroleum companies, who claimed that the federal Comprehensive Environmental Response, Compensation, and

Liability Act of 1980 (CERCLA) precluded state efforts to duplicate the purposes of the federal legislation (Lieber, 1983, p. 69). At a minimum, such federal/state tensions have the effect of delaying or postponing actions to improve the quality of the environment.

Perhaps the most salient problem advocates of national environmental policies want to address is the lack of uniform standards from state to state. In the absence of a strong federal role in environmental policy, many states will simply opt to do little to improve and protect the environment. When federal programs were directed toward providing technical assistance and financing, state and local governments tended not to work toward achieving reductions in air pollution, water pollution, and so on. To such advocates, if the environment is to be improved, the federal government will have to impose that goal on the states. Yet there is abundant evidence that when the federal government imposes uniform pollution standards, the result is not necessarily improved environmental conditions. Indeed, at times, such uniform standards actually impede states that would otherwise be able to act on their own. For example, in his evaluation of the 1972 Federal Water Pollution Control Act Amendments, Lieber argues that "as a result of the Act's uniform requirements, Wyoming will be forced to needlessly install sophisticated [water] monitoring devices, and Texas, which already has a well-developed planning program, will have to unnecessarily reshuffle this function" (Lieber, 1975, p. 191).

Additionally, the relationship between the federal agencies and the states is influenced by the presidential administration. Changes in administrations can have a substantial effect on how the EPA defines its mission, and consequently how the EPA decides to interact with state and local governments. To be sure, there have been times when EPA officials seemed to be less interested in environmental protection than in stimulating economic growth and development. During such a period, there is much less effort to impose federal standards on states. Consequently, there tends to be less tension over matters of environmental regulation. At the same time, however, states wanting the EPA to be more aggressive in environmental implementation may find an unresponsive agency. For example, during the early Reagan administration, many states expressed frustration with the lack of federal action to clean up Superfund priority hazardous waste sites (Cohen, 1984).

The challenge from a perspective of federalism is for Congress and the EPA to develop pollution control policies that have substantial flexibility to account for variations in needs from one state to another, without creating loopholes for recalcitrant states that want to avoid complying. This has proven to be a formidable challenge, but not one from which Congress and the EPA have shied.

A Summary of the Role of Government in the Environment

This chapter suggests that the governmental role in the environment derives from the broadly defined policy-making process. This process, often characterized as being composed of problem formation, policy formulation and agenda setting, policy legitimation and adoption, implementation, and evaluation, involves a variety of actors. Included at different stages of the process at the federal level are members of Congress, especially its environmentally oriented committees, several administrative agencies, the courts, and major interest groups.

Perhaps the single most important stage of the policy-making process to understand, in the federal role in environmental policy, is implementation. A number of federal agencies, most notably the EPA, OSHA, and FDA, perform regulatory functions with direct environmental implications. To varying degrees, all three agencies perform a rule-making function—issuing regulations that must be followed as a matter of law. Each agency makes decisions about these regulations through a different process within the broad requirements of the Administrative Procedures Act.

Regulations issued by EPA and other agencies frequently rely on technical and scientific information in the form of risk assessment. These risk assessments attempt to estimate the level of danger that particular environmental contaminants pose for people who might be exposed to them. Risk assessments have become increasingly important components of the regulatory decision process. It has been suggested that the full range of priorities in environmental regulation be driven by formal assessments of risk. In this way, efforts by EPA would be concentrated on those areas that would produce the most benefit to people. At the same time, however, many people are skeptical of the idea that risk assessment can ever be so flawlessly conducted as to render more explicitly value-laden judgments unnecessary.

Various federal environmental programs involve substantial intergovernmental effort. Especially in the implementation process, the EPA may work with state and local governments. While this intergovernmental administration process sometimes consists of nothing more than federal provision of technical and financial assistance to state and local governments, it can also at times lead to a great deal of tension and controversy. Efforts to impose federal implementation standards on states may prevent states from making environmental improvements and may require states to take actions that produce little or no environmental improvement. Efforts to pursue more flexible federal strategies often provide some states with the ability to achieve major environmental improvements, but could also allow less-aggressive states to avoid complying.

With the general picture of the role of government in the environment in mind, it is now time to examine specific environmental policies. The next chapter focuses on the nature of public policies toward air pollution. Issues such as whether and how policies have tried to reduce or prevent air pollution and related problems, including acid rain and global warming, are investigated. In the subsequent chapter, the focus is on water pollution policy. And in the final chapter, the subject centers on toxic and hazardous waste policy. In each of these applications, the specific patterns of policy-making, policy results, and related controversies are explicitly examined.

3

Public Policies to Protect
and Improve the Air Quality
of the Nation and the World

Chapter 1 discussed a wide variety of current and emerging problems thought to be related to air pollution. In this discussion, it was clear that there are some very real disagreements about whether specific air pollution-related problems actually are problems. There is some disagreement about whether acid rain is a problem. There is disagreement about whether there is any such thing as the greenhouse effect, and if so, whether it actually is a problem. But just as there is debate about whether these issues constitute problems, there is perhaps even greater disagreement concerning what, if anything, should be done about these problems. In this chapter, the focus is on the efforts that have been made to reduce or avoid air pollution problems, and the debates that have been associated with these efforts.

There is probably no set of environmental problems that has received more federal public policy attention than air pollution. Air quality issues became the source of major public concern in America during the 1960s, when recurring air quality crises threatened the health and welfare of people in various places around the country. Since that time, the federal role in air pollution policy has steadily evolved, and in many

ways has served as a forerunner for public policies in other environmental areas. In the early 1970s there were attempts to enact truly
innovative policies to improve air quality. Yet these attempts provide
examples of what happens when expectations about what can be accomplished through federal legislation far exceed existing capabilities and
technologies. Legislation sought to achieve extremely ambitious improvements in air quality, and even prescribed goals that no one knew
how to achieve at that time. This conclusion perhaps contributed to a
period in the early 1980s when expectations seemed to diminish, when
air pollution policy did not seem to be accorded quite the high priority
it previously had.

In more recent times, however, efforts at improving air quality have
been redoubled, partly because of increasing recognition not only that
air pollution persists, but also that it creates other major environmental
and public health problems. As noted in Chapter 1, air pollution contributes to acid rain, which in turn creates other problems, such as
damage to forests and animal life. Air pollution very probably contributes to the greenhouse effect or global warming, and the depletion of
the ozone layer of the earth's atmosphere, which could very well create
another set of threats to the world's ecology. Concern has also been
stimulated by the recognition that air pollution creates truly global
problems—that the effects of air pollution are not necessarily confined
to a single nation or political jurisdiction.

Tackling problems of air pollution is no small technical task, but from
a political perspective the task is even more daunting—for at least two
major reasons. First, the jurisdiction or party that pollutes the air is often
not the party that experiences the consequences of that pollution. When
major industries in the midwestern part of the United States engage in
emitting air pollution, the effects might be most pronounced in New
England or even in Canada. When developers engage in burning the rain
forests in Brazil, the effects might be most immediately felt somewhere
else. However, efforts at addressing air pollution from an international
perspective are motivated by an increasing recognition that air pollution
and its effects are global issues—they affect everyone. Even as air
pollution is increasingly recognized as a global problem, there are still
economic interests that prefer to trade short-term economic gain for the
more dispersed negative ecological consequences.

Indeed, the second major reason why the politics of air pollution
policy constitutes a particular challenge is that it runs headlong into
issues of economic development and growth, and the energy independence

necessary to create this growth. For example, because much of the damaging air pollution is emitted as a result of fossil fuel burned by electric generating plants, reductions can only come as a result of either: (a) changing to types of fuel that don't pollute as much, generally non-domestic coal and petroleum products; (b) installing very expensive equipment to clean the polluted air before it is discharged, which increases domestic costs of production; or (c) reducing the amount of power produced, which stifles economic development. These are the types of problems that contemporary air pollution policy must overcome.

This chapter provides an introduction to some of the major controversies in America's air pollution policy since the early 1960s. It starts by presenting a review of efforts to enact and implement air pollution programs—designed to improve and protect the quality of the air. This review will reveal some laudable attempts to effect air quality improvements that, in the final analysis, probably did not work very well. It suggests that during the 1980s, the apparent failures of these earlier attempts were frequently used as excuses for not doing more to diminish air pollution. It also traces the efforts to reformulate air pollution policy, with emphasis on efforts to overcome the inertia from the 1980s by pursuing new federal legislation that would rectify some of the problems with earlier policy. In reviewing the actions of the federal government, it will become clear that many of the clashes of values described in Chapter 1 have created significant political impediments, preventing greater efforts to improve air quality. But first, a brief review of federal air pollution legislation (a list of which is presented in Table 3.1) and programs is in order.

Air Pollution Legislation Since 1955

The first federal legislation explicitly focusing on air pollution was the Air Pollution Control Act of 1955. By today's standards, this Act did extraordinarily little to actually work toward clean air. It limited the federal role in air pollution policy, and relegated to state and local government all responsibility for cleaning up the air or preventing air pollution. The federal role consisted of providing technical research and support to state and local governments. What perhaps makes this Act a notable first step in the fight against air pollution is that it recognized

Table 3.1 Major Federal Air Pollution Legislation Since 1955

The Air Pollution Control Act of 1955
The Air Pollution Control Act Amendments of 1960
   (The Schenck Act of 1960)
The Air Pollution Control Act Amendments of 1962
The Clean Air Act of 1963
The Motor-Vehicle Air Pollution Control Act of 1965
The Air Quality Act of 1967
   (The National Emission Standards Act of 1967)
The Clean Air Act Amendments of 1970
The Clean Air Act Amendments of 1977
The National Acid Precipitation Act of 1980
   (Part of the Energy Security Act of 1980)
The Air Pollution Act of 1990

---

the idea that air pollution was an emerging national problem. The hope was that if federal legislation pointed to air pollution as a serious emerging problem, state and local governments would take air quality control initiatives.

Concern about air pollution, and state and local government inaction on air quality, prompted Congress to try again. The Air Pollution Control Act Amendments of 1960 and 1962 added to the recognition of air pollution as a growing problem, but did no more to directly improve air quality than the preceding legislation. The 1960 Amendments (sometimes called the Schenck Act, after its congressional sponsor) asked the Surgeon General to determine whether motor vehicle exhaust was detrimental to human health. The Surgeon General's initial studies apparently convinced Congress to amend the Air Pollution Control Act in 1962. The Surgeon General's final reports demonstrated the need for somewhat more federal action against air pollution. Thus, Congress embarked on a more elaborate legislative change the very next year.

The first major federal action on air pollution occurred in 1963, with the enactment of the Clean Air Act. This Act started with the premise that air pollution was essentially a state and local problem. The federal role in air pollution control continued to be quite limited, providing essentially no authority for any federal agency to take actions unless requested by a state. Rosenbaum (1977, p. 140) suggests that, in the air pollution legislation through 1963, deference to "state authority was virtually a prescription for inaction. Few states were eager to write or enforce stringent pollution controls . . . [because they were] . . . eager to lure industries" to provide jobs and economic development. Despite this general underlying philosophy, this Act made far more detailed efforts to seek federal-state-local cooperation and encourage the automobile industry to take voluntary actions to limit the pollution emissions of their cars.

The limited federal role started to change with the enactment of the 1965 Motor-Vehicle Air Pollution Control Act and the 1967 Air Quality Act. The Motor-Vehicle Air Pollution Control Act focused on the persistent problem of pollution emissions from automobiles. Increasing evidence from research pointed to automobiles as major contributors to air pollution, and health research suggested that the components of car exhaust indeed created significant health risks. This Act was to be implemented by the Department of Health, Education, and Welfare (HEW) (there was not yet a federal Environmental Protection Agency), and required the secretary of this department to establish emission standards for new motor vehicles. It was largely as the result of HEW's efforts on behalf of this law that, starting in 1968, new cars were required to have pollution control equipment to reduce by 90% the hydrocarbon and carbon dioxide emissions from cars. HEW also required automobile manufacturers to have new cars certified as meeting the federal standards before the cars could be sold.

The Air Quality Act of 1967 (sometimes referred to as the National Emission Standards Act) was apparently a response to the recognition that the states were not taking much initiative toward improving air quality. In this legislation, Congress took an incremental step in trying to push the states into action by requiring them to establish air quality districts or regions, to set standards and control procedures for each district, and to formulate plans specifying how these standards and control procedures would be implemented and enforced. The federal government was given responsibility for recommending to the states what technologies should be used to meet the states' specific regional air quality standards. But by 1970 it became clear that neither the states nor the federal government was able to make much progress toward improving air quality. When the 1967 Act had been debated, there was much discussion about the idea of establishing federal national air quality standards, but the final Act merely provided for the study of the concept of such standards.

Perhaps out of frustration with the lack of progress, Congress embarked in 1970 on an ambitious path of action, which helped set the direction for federal air pollution policy even today. This occurred with the adoption of the Clean Air Act Amendments of 1970. Although the title of the Act suggests incremental changes, this legislation marked a very new and different approach to air pollution control. It was also the first piece of federal pollution control legislation turned over to the new Environmental Protection Agency (EPA) for implementation. The Act called for EPA to establish national air quality standards for designated pollutants, rather than relying on state-determined district standards. The Act required EPA to set primary standards, which would specify maximum allowable levels of "criteria pollutants" to protect the public from immediate health damage, to be achieved by 1975; and secondary standards, which would specify pollutant levels to protect the more general environment from any adverse health effects, to be achieved "within a reasonable time." Criteria pollutants consist of emissions that become ubiquitous (broadly dispersed) in the environment, and include specifically sulfur dioxide, nitrogen oxides, lead, ozone, carbon monoxide, and particulate matter. These primary and secondary air quality standards are referred to as the National Ambient Air Quality Standards. The specific standards, and the implementation of these standards, will be discussed in more detail later.

The 1970 Clean Air Act Amendments also required that all states submit to EPA, by the beginning of 1972, plans to put into effect the standards set by EPA. These plans were to specify exactly how each state intended to achieve air quality that met the EPA's standards by prescribed periods of time. Automobiles were once again the target of regulatory efforts. Automobile manufacturers were required to build cars by 1975 that emitted 90% less hydrocarbon and carbon monoxide in 1975 than in 1970, and 90% less nitrogen oxide in 1976 than in 1970. This Act also contained what are called "non-degradation" provisions, which essentially stipulate that if a local district's air is cleaner than federal standards allow, the air quality cannot be allowed to degrade even if the dirtier air is still cleaner than permitted by the federal standards. It also provided the EPA with enforcement powers not previously in place. With this law, EPA could take direct action against violators of the air emissions standards, rather than relying on the states for enforcement. In extreme situations, such as pollution emergencies, the EPA was empowered to order enforcement against specific violators and was allowed to take civil actions, including imposition of stiff fines and prison sentences for violators.

The 1970 Act also called for controlling new sources of air pollution in the form of 14 specific pollutants (called toxic emissions) coming from 19 specified industries. These toxic emissions included arsenic, barium, boron, chlorine gas, chromium, copper, hydrogen chloride, manganese, selenium, vanadium, zinc, pesticides, and radioactive substances. Newly constructed facilities would no longer be permitted to emit these substances. The Act did not attempt to affect emissions of these substances from already existing facilities. However, it did define several hazardous agents, including lead, mercury, asbestos, and cadmium, limitations on which would apply to all facilities, new or existing.

The 1970 Clean Air Act was amended in 1977, with most of the amendments simply changing the dates by which compliance would be required. For example, the deadlines for automobiles to meet hydrocarbon and carbon monoxide standards were extended. It also made the standard for automobile nitric oxide emissions less strict. These amendments clarified the degradation provisions of the 1970 Act, creating three categories of air quality districts based on how much degradation would be tolerated in the future. Tolerance of future degradation was largely a function of how polluted the air already was. Some air quality districts were classified as Class I, where no deterioration would be permitted; Class II, where moderate degradation would be allowed; and Class III, where substantial degradation could occur. In no case would degradation be permitted to produce air that did not meet the air quality standards. These degradation standards carried with them clear implications for economic and industrial development. In the Class I areas, virtually no new economic development would be permitted. In Class II areas, some carefully regulated economic development could occur. And in Class III areas, air pollution was considered so insignificant a problem that economic development could proceed without the need to worry about exceeding air quality standards. The Clean Air Act of 1970 and its 1977 Amendments have created the core of America's national air pollution policy.

At the same time the 1977 Amendments were adopted, Congress established the National Commission on Air Quality, an organization independent of the EPA, to assess and evaluate the EPA's implementation of the Amendments. It was also charged with recommending future amendments and legislation that would help achieve cleaner air. In other words, Congress created an agency to oversee and monitor another agency. The later description of the implementation of the 1977 Amendments provides a specific example of a situation in which this National Commission was quite critical of the EPA.

Although there was increasing concern about air quality and consequences of air pollution over the next 13 years, no new action legislation was enacted. Congress did enact the National Acid Precipitation Act of 1980 (part of the Energy Security Act of 1980), which, among other things not directly related to air pollution, created a Federal Interagency Task Force on Acid Precipitation. This interagency task force was composed of people from the U.S. Departments of Agriculture, Energy, Interior, Commerce, Health and Human Services, and State; the National Oceanic and Atmospheric Administration; the President's Council on Environmental Quality; the National Aeronautics and Space Administration; the National Science Foundation; the Tennessee Valley Authority; and representatives from several federal research laboratories (NAPAP, 1990, p. 2). This interagency task force then created the National Acid Precipitation Assessment Program (NAPAP), referred to briefly in Chapter 1. NAPAP received the full budget appropriated by Congress, anticipated to be some $50 million over 10 years. It actually spent about 10 times that amount to conduct, and subsequently provide the most comprehensive assessment of, research on acid rain.

Starting in 1981, however, with the inauguration of President Reagan, a new philosophy toward federal regulation took hold. This philosophy dictated that there should be less, rather than more, federal involvement in regulation. Although the 1977 Clean Air Act Amendments were still in effect, the funding of this Act was due to expire in September of 1981. The Reagan administration made some initial efforts to get Congress to essentially repeal national air quality standards, to totally eliminate federal sanctions against air quality regions not meeting the national standards, and to drop the requirement that cars maintain working air pollution control devices (Tobin, 1984, p. 232). For a variety of reasons, Congress declined to enact such legislative revisions, and funding for the 1977 Amendments was continued. Instead, Reagan administration efforts turned to changing the way existing law was implemented by EPA, as will be discussed later. As an alternative, the Reagan administration opted to call for the federal role in air pollution to revert to its earlier position—one of conducting research. Action on problems such as acid rain and global warming were deferred, yielding to the call for more research to understand these problems. Many people, especially those in environmental interest groups, read the shift in attention to research as an effort to delay, perhaps indefinitely, further federal air regulation (Regens & Rycroft, 1988, p. 30).

By the late 1980s it became clear that existing law did not provide sufficient foundation for addressing some of the more important air pollution problems. It also became clear that calls for more research as a substitute for directed action were an inadequate response to air pollution problems. The NAPAP, for example, had issued numerous reports documenting the probable causes of, and a variety of different environmental effects from, acid rain. In 1989, the Bush administration proposed major changes in clean air legislation that represented an "acknowledgement that the existing Clean Air Act was not suited to dealing with the problem" of acid rain (Leaf, 1990, p. 28). This proposal served as the basis for enactment of the Clean Air Act of 1990, which became the first major attempt since 1970 to not only provide a broader range of coverage but also create a solid statutory foundation for EPA actions to specifically battle acid rain, the greenhouse effect, and thinning of the ozone layer (Schneider, 1990). This was accomplished by including in the new legislation a variety of new goals and methods for achieving these goals.

This Act's provisions require that sulfur dioxide emissions be reduced by 10 million tons per year, representing a 50% reduction by the year 2000. After the year 2000, sulfur dioxide emissions would be capped so that they would remain constant. This provision is aimed largely at conventional (coal-burning) electric generating plants, mostly in the East and the Midwest, which burn high-sulfur coal to produce the power. (A list of the target plants is found in Table 3.4, discussed later.) The 1990 Clean Air Act also calls for reductions in pollution from automobile exhaust, with specific polluting components of the exhaust to be reduced between 30% and 60% between 1994 and 1998. Additionally, the Act requires cities to comply with clean air standards in 5 to 20 years, depending on the severity of the air pollution problem. Cities not meeting the standards in the specified period of time would potentially have the air cleanup programs taken over by the EPA.

The 1990 Act also targets industrial air pollution for specific reductions. American industries were emitting approximately 2.7 million tons of cancer-causing pollutants into the air every year. Under previous law, only seven of the hundreds of known cancer-causing pollutants emitted by industry were subjected to EPA regulations. Under the 1990 Act, 189 of the most dangerous chemical pollutants would be regulated by the EPA. A list of these pollutants is found in Table 3.2. The Act specifies that emissions of these substances must be reduced by 90% by the year 2000. It also calls for a total phaseout of the major ozone-depleting chlorofluorocarbons, or CFCs, by the year 2000.

Perhaps the most innovative aspect of this law is the development of a pollution credit or coupon system as a form of pollution trading.

Table 3.2 Hazardous Air Pollutants as Specified in the Clean Air Act of 1990

Chemical Name	*Chemical Name*
Acetaldehyde	o-Cresol
Acetamide	m-Cresol
Acetonitrile	p-Cresol
Acetophenone	Cumene
2-Acetylaminofluorene	2,4-D, salts and esters
Acrolein	DDE
Acrylamide	Diazomethane
Acrylic acid	Dibenzofurans
Acrylonitrile	1,2-Dibromo-3-chloropropane
Allyl chloride	Dibutylphthalate
4-Aminobiphenyl	1,4-Dichlorobenzene(p)
Aniline	3,3-Dichlorobenzidene
o-Anisidine	Dichloroethyl ether
Asbestos	(Bis(2-chloroethyl)ether)
Benzene (including from gasoline)	1,3-Dichloropropene
Benzidine	Dichlorvos
Benzotrichloride	Diethanolamine
Benzyl chloride	N,N-Diethyl aniline
Biphenyl	(N,N-Dimethylaniline)
Bis(2-ethylhexyl) phthalate (DEHP)	Diethyl sulfate
Bis(chloromethyl)ether	3,3-Dimethoxybenzidine
Bromoform	Dimethyl aminoazobenzene
1,3-Butadiene	3,3-Dimethyl benzidine
Calcium cyanamide	Dimethyl carbamoyl chloride
Caprolactam	Dimethyl formamide
Captan	1,1-Dimethyl hydrazine
Carbaryl	Dimethyl phthalate
Carbon disulfide	Dimethyl sulfate
Carbon tetrachloride	4,6-Dinitro-o-cresol, and salts
Carbonyl sulfide	2,4-Dinitrophenol
Catechol	2,4-Dinitrotoluene
Chloramben	1,4-Dioxane (1,4-Diethyleneoxide)
Chlordane	1,2-Diphenylhydrazine
Chlorine	Epichlorohydrin
Chloroacetic acid	(1-Chloro-2,3-epoxypropane)
2-Chloroacetophenone	1,2-Epoxybutane
Chlorobenzene	Ethyl acrylate
Chlorobenzilate	Ethyl benzene
Chloroform	Ethyl carbamate (Urethane)
Chloromethyl methyl ether	Ethyl chloride (Chloroethane)
Chloroprene	Ethylene dibromide (Dibromoethane)
Cresols/Cresylic acid (isomers and	Ethylene dichloride (1,2-Dichloroethane)
mixture)	Ethylene glycol

continued

Table 3.2 Continued

Chemical Name	Chemical Name
Ethylene imine (Aziridine)	N-Nitroso-N-methylurea
Ethylene oxide	N-Nitrosodimethylamine
Ethylene thiourea	N-Nitrosomorpholine
Ethylidene dichloride	Parathion
(1,1-Dichloroethane)	Pentachloronitrobenzene (Quintobenzene)
Formaldehyde	Pentachlorophenol
Heptachlor	Phenol
Hexachlorobenzene	p-Phenylenediamine
Hexachlorobutadiene	Phosgene
Hexachlorocyclopentadiene	Phosphine
Hexachloroethane	Phosphorus
Hexamethylene-1,6-diisocyanate	Phthalic anhydride
Hexamethylphosphoramide	Polychlorinated biphenyls (Aroclors)
Hexane	1,3-Propane sultone
Hydrazine	beta-Propiolactone
Hydrochloric acid	Propionaldehyde
Hydrogen fluoride (hydrofluoric acid)	Propoxur (Baygon)
Hydroquinone	Propylene dichloride
Isophorone	(1,2-Dichloropropane)
Lindane (all isomers)	Propylene oxide
Maleic anhydride	1,2-Propylenimine (2-Methyl aziridine)
Methanol	Quinoline
Methoxychlor	Quinone
Methyl bromide (Bromomethane)	Styrene
Methyl chloride (Chloromethane)	Styrene oxide
Methyl chloroform	2,3,7,8-Tetrachlorodibenzo-p-dioxin
(1,1,1-Trichloroethane)	1,1,2,2-Tetrachloroethane
Methyl ethyl ketone (2-Butanone)	Tetrachloroethylene (Perchloroethylene)
Methyl hydrazine	Titanium tetrachloride
Methyl iodide (Iodomethane)	Toluene
Methyl isobutyl ketone (Hexone)	2,4-Toluene diamine
Methyl isocyanate	2,4-Toluene diisocyanate
Methyl methacrylate	o-Toluidine
Methyl tert butyl ether	Toxaphene (chlorinated camphene)
4,4-Methylene bis(2-chloroaniline)	1,2,4-Trichlorobenzene
Methylene chloride (Dichloromethane)	1,1,2-Trichloroethane
Methylene diphenyl diisocyanate (MDI)	Trichloroethylene
4,4-Methylenedianiline	2,4,5-Trichlorophenol
Naphthalene	2,4,6-Trichlorophenol
Nitrobenzene	Triethylamine
4-Nitrobiphenyl	Trifluralin
4-Nitrophenol	2,2,4-Trimethylpentane
2-Nitropropane	Vinyl acetate

continued

Table 3.2 Continued

Chemical Name	Chemical Name
Vinyl bromide	Chromium compounds
Vinyl chloride	Cobalt compounds
Vinylidene chloride	Coke oven emissions
(1,1-Dichloroethylene)	Cyanide compounds
Xylenes (isomers and mixture)	Glycci ethers
o-Xylenes	Lead compounds
m-Xylenes	Manganese compounds
p-Xylenes	Mercury compounds
Antimony compounds	Mineral fibers
Arsenic compounds (inorganic including	Nickel compounds
arsine)	Polycytis organic matter
Beryllium compounds	Radionuclides (including radon)
Cadmium compounds	Selenium compounds

SOURCE: PL101-549, Sec. 112 (11)(b)(1), November 15, 1990.

Polluting industries are issued coupons that allow them to emit a certain maximum amount of specific pollutants. In other words, facilities are allocated permissible pollution levels. An industrial facility that takes action to reduce air pollution emissions and does not "use up" its allocation can actually sell the remaining portion to other facilities. A specific polluting manufacturing facility could decide to spend money to install the technology to remove pollutants from the air before being expelled, thereby allowing it to sell its excess to the highest bidder, or it could buy some other facility's excess polluting capacity instead. The idea underlying this system is that industries can decide for themselves which course of action of compliance is cheapest, and pursue this course without necessarily making the air more polluted than it otherwise would be.

The idea of pollution trading as associated with the use of coupons or credits is not a new idea. Indeed, economists have been advocating pollution trading systems for many years. However, such credits were not used previously as a matter of public policy, except as part of the EPA's "bubble" policy, as described later. Environmentalists had, for many years, opposed the use of such coupons because it was thought to be tantamount to issuance of a license or a right to pollute. The position of many environmentalists has been that a goal of no pollution—zero discharges—is the only rational anti-pollution policy to pursue, so it was quite difficult for them to accept the idea that specific industrial facilities would be given a right to pollute, and that they could actually sell this right to other firms. Mechanisms to allow pollution trading have also been criticized because they are thought to be very difficult to enforce; there is little evidence that their use would actually improve the quality of the environment; and it is doubtful that the implementation of these mechanisms can be flexible enough to not impede economic growth and still avoid abuse (Liroff, 1986, pp. 9-18). However, the economic rationale for trying this system seems quite strong.

The discussion of the policy-making processes, as presented later, suggests that one of the reasons why it took some 13 years to enact legislation more directly addressing contemporary air pollution problems is that there was serious disagreement about the best way to proceed. Until environmental advocates were willing to accept pollution credits, there was not sufficient support in Congress to pass new legislation. The idea of pollution trading and related issues will be addressed more fully in the later discussion of the evolution of the federal government's air pollution "bubble" policy.

The Processes of Making Federal Air Pollution Policy

It is not uncommon to apply a policy-making process framework, as described in Chapter 2, to individual pieces of legislation. Indeed, the policy-making process associated with the Clean Air Act of 1970 is described in some detail below. However, that same framework can also be applied to a much lengthier period of time where, for a given piece of legislation, the problem formation, policy adoption and legitimation processes are characterized by legislative actions of 10 or 15 years before. This is the way the policy-making process associated with the Clean Air Act of 1970 has been described by Charles O. Jones (1975) in his study of air pollution policy-making.

The Making of Air Pollution Policy: The Clean Air Act of 1970

The discussions of the various pieces of federal legislation since 1955 briefly alluded to some of the major events and actors surrounding each legislative enactment. These descriptions suggested that the Clean Air Act of 1970 ushered in something of a new era in air pollution policy, at least with respect to the prescribed role of the federal government vis-à-vis state and local governments in setting and enforcing air quality standards. Logical questions that might arise out of this are: What happened inside and outside of Congress to make this change happen? Why were decisions made to have the federal government embark on very ambitious and, some would say, unreasonable and unattainable air pollution goals? Additionally, one might wonder whether this new and ambitious piece of legislation actually was implemented consistently with the legislation. A related question is whether, as a consequence of the law, the quality of the air improved as much as was required by the law. Answers to these questions are found, at least in part, in an examination of the policy-making process associated with this legislation.

The Problem Formation Process

By 1970 there was a clearly developing sense of urgency about air pollution. As described earlier, this urgency stemmed in part from an increasing incidence of air pollution crisis events, such as those that occurred during air inversions in the city of Pittsburgh. As Jones (1975, pp. 137-155) notes, by the late 1960s, public awareness and concern about air pollution had grown markedly, largely because of people's observations of air quality deterioration. Additionally, as a result of increased emphasis on health effects research, especially investigations by the Surgeon General, it became increasingly clear that air pollution was not benign. Rather, increased air pollution seemed to be associated with many serious health consequences. But these events alone do not fully explain why Congress decided to embark upon such a significantly different approach to air pollution policy.

An additional and critical explanation of the Clean Air Act's more aggressive approach has to do with the results of earlier legislation. Although the 1967 Air Quality Act required states to develop air quality regions and implementation plans, by 1970 no state had a federally approved implementation plan (Rosenbaum, 1977, p. 141). It became clear that the earlier legislation was neither handled in a timely manner by the federal government nor complied with by state and local governments. In air pollution control legislation from the mid-1950s, Congress had started nudging the states into taking action against pollution. Each successive piece of legislation took a rather incremental step to get state and local governments to act. As little progress was made, additional steps were taken until 1967, when legislation required specific actions by states. Just as most states declined to take these actions, the federal agency with responsibility for reviewing state air quality standards and implementation plans (the National Air Pollution Control Administration in the Department of Health, Education, and Welfare) was very slow to decide which standards and plans to approve (Jones, 1975, pp. 117-139). By 1970 it was clear to many that additional administrative resources were needed, and the states would have to be pushed rather than nudged.

The Policy Formulation and Adoption Process

Given an apparent desire on the part of many members of Congress to seek more effective means for improving air quality, work began in 1969 on formulating new legislation to accomplish this goal. The members of Congress who took some initiative in developing clean air legislation were Edmund Muskie (D-Maine), chairman since 1963 of the Air and Water Pollution Subcommittee of the Senate Public Works Committee, and Paul Rogers (D-Florida), the second ranking member of the Subcommittee on Public Health and Welfare of the House Interstate and Foreign Commerce Committee. At that time, the House had no committee or subcommittee dedicated to pollution issues. Muskie, who had built something of a reputation as an environmental advocate, nevertheless had for some years maintained the position that pollution legislation had to be principally focused on state authority rather than federal authority.

A number of factors determined the sequence of events surrounding the formulation of the Clean Air Act. First, Edmund Muskie, who had taken a personal interest in environmental issues, became embroiled in a dispute with Henry Jackson (D-Washington), the chairman of the Senate Interior and Insular Affairs Committee, a dispute that apparently had more to do with personalities and jurisdiction than with the substance of anti-pollution legislation (Jones, 1975, p. 57). Second, in May 1970 the Ralph Nader study group on air pollution released a report that was extremely critical of Muskie's previous efforts on air pollution, especially the 1967 Act. This report referred to Muskie as "the Chief architect of the disastrous Air Quality Act of 1967 . . . [and] . . . the Senator's passivity since 1967 in the face of an ever worsening air pollution crisis compounds his earlier failure" (Jones, 1975, p. 192). Third, Muskie was up for reelection in 1970, and apparently entertained the possibility of running for president in 1972, both of which had something of a distracting effect.

When the Senate finally began formulating new air pollution legislation, the effort was very much bipartisan, with a number of Democrats and Republicans from the Muskie Subcommittee more directly involved than Muskie himself. Added to this was the fact that the House of Representatives had started work on new legislation somewhat earlier. Paul Rogers took the initiative in the House, even though he had not previously done much to establish any record in pollution policy. Apparently, the main reason why Rogers took a sudden interest in air pollution was that he disliked Muskie and wanted to help steal his thunder, and because Rogers faced a major reelection challenge. Consequently, the House of Representatives played a stronger role in the development of this air pollution legislation than it had in previous clean air legislation.

Additionally, the Nixon administration also took some initiative by proposing national air quality standards, along with stricter automobile exhaust emissions standards and enforcement. Not to be outdone by the Nixon administration, Representative Rogers managed to have legislation introduced into the House that contained more stringent air pollution provisions than the administration proposal. And not to be outdone by the House, Muskie saw to it that the Senate air pollution bill was stricter yet. Jones (1975, pp. 203-205) describes this process as "policy escalation." Even though this policy escalation seems clearly present, when the Senate House Conference met to iron out differences between the House and Senate versions of the bill, there was considerable pressure from various industry lobbyists to weaken the law. This, of course, is not unusual. However, according to Jones, what was unusual was the fact that, perhaps for the first time, there was also lobbying from environmental groups, so that lobbying by industries was countered by lobbying on behalf of environmental protection.

The result was the passage of a bill that was heavily influenced by the Senate version, carried considerably stricter standards, and was more aggressive than any of its predecessors. The resulting law carried provisions that, in Jones' words, were beyond the immediate capabilities of anyone to implement them. Jones refers to these features collectively as "speculative augmentation," suggesting that the previous law had been augmented by nothing more than wishful and hypothetical ideas about what could actually be accomplished. In terms of the dynamics of Congress, the resulting law reestablished Muskie as the king of the air pollution politics.

**Difficulties in Implementing
National Clean Air Policy**

Criticisms of America's public policies toward clean air have focused on many problems, but inevitably such criticisms begin by examining the implementation process. Whether because the original legislation was badly conceived or worded, or because the implementing agency was incompetent, ill-prepared, or questionably motivated, the implementation processes reveal the true character of clean air policy. This becomes apparent through a review of how the Clean Air Act of 1970 and its 1977 Amendments were put into effect. This review reveals that there have been times when implementation has been pursued relatively aggressively, and other times when agencies have backed away from rigorous application.

Implementation of the 1970 Clean Air Act

There have been very few pieces of federal legislation subjected to as much and as varied criticism as the Clean Air Act of 1970. Almost all of these criticisms point to some aspect of implementation as a problem. Very often such criticisms conclude that implementation was made difficult or impossible by some aspect of the law itself. This section will try to accomplish three tasks. First, it will explain how the implementation of the Clean Air Act was to take place, as specified under the law. Second, it will explain how the Act was actually implemented. And third, it will focus on areas where actual practice did not meet prescribed implementation. This results in a clearer picture, which shows that because of implementation problems, the quality of the air in many places around the country was not improved as much as the law had anticipated.

As noted earlier, this Act specifies a strategy designed to achieve pollutant-specific air quality standards by specific dates. The standards, to be developed and issued by the EPA, were to specify maximum allowable concentrations of common pollutants emitted into the air. There were to be two separate sets of standards: a more strict set aimed at protecting public health (primary standards), and a less strict set aimed at protecting and preserving public welfare (secondary standards). Once these standards were issued, it was up to each state to take primary implementation responsibility, which included creating a state implementation plan describing exactly how all of the state's air quality regions would meet the primary standards by the deadline of mid-1975. The law required all states to submit these implementation plans within 9 months of the EPA's issuance of standards. Subsequent state responsibilities included issuing permits to existing polluters specifying how much of what kinds of pollutants they could emit, and how much reduction in these pollutants was required; monitoring compliance of polluters with the conditions of their permits; taking actions against violators to get them to comply; and issuing permits for new polluting sources, such as new factories.

The EPA apparently had little difficulty formulating and issuing its initial set of ambient air quality standards, which it did in April of 1971. The primary standards specify both the maximum allowable concentrations of six pollutants and a period of time to which these concentrations apply. Sometimes there are two different primary standards for the same pollutant, one applying to a short period of time and the other to a longer period. For example, there are two primary standards for sulfur dioxide emissions, one applying to the average over an entire year, and the other applying to any given 24-hour period. The former standard specifies that average sulfur dioxide emissions over a year cannot exceed 0.03 parts per million (or 80 micrograms per cubic milliliter of air), and in any 24-hour period sulfur dioxide emissions cannot exceed 0.14 parts per million (the equivalent of 365 micrograms per cubic milliliter of air). The federal and state efforts to enforce these standards will be discussed shortly.

Once these standards were issued, the states were given 9 months to submit their implementation plans—proposals specifying how each of the 247 air quality regions was going to meet these standards by 1975. Facing the need to comply with this requirement, yet often not having the technical capacity to base the plans on very accurate information, many states submitted plans that were sometimes too strict, and sometimes too lenient on specific polluters. According to Liroff (1986, pp. 21-23), the state implementation plans were based on estimates of how polluted the air already was, according to existing monitors of ambient air quality, and simple estimates of the percentage reduction in emissions needed to achieve the specific national standards. Then the states would examine the existing sources of air pollution, decide which of these needed to be regulated, and make some guesses about which technologies could best be used to reduce each source's emissions. The states had very little ability to determine whether a given stationary source of pollution actually contributed to the ambient air quality, and merely assumed that if specific polluters' emissions were reduced, ambient air quality would improve accordingly. Practically no state had the time or ability to estimate with any accuracy what compliance with the state plan would mean to the economy.

Once completed, the implementation plan was then submitted to EPA for review and approval. As the EPA made its final decisions to accept state plans, various parties, believing their interests were not being served, looked to the courts for redress. Industries and industry groups often felt that their state's plan should have been disapproved because it was too restrictive. Many polluters in the private sector filed federal lawsuits against EPA, believing that they would be driven out of business if they had to spend the money to comply with the state plan. Environmentalists, on the other hand, frequently felt that the state plans too often catered to economic interests rather than seeking to protect air quality. So they started filing federal lawsuits, claiming that the plans should have been disapproved because they were too lenient on polluters. Disagreements and efforts to effect change resulted in a total inability to meet the 1975 deadline. According to the U.S. Council on Environmental Quality (1975, p. 59), not one state implementation plan had received final approval from the EPA by 1975.

Implementation of the Clean Air Act's auto emissions control provisions provides another view of the problems faced by the EPA. The initial EPA strategy was to focus on new cars, guaranteeing that successive generations of new models would produce increasingly less carbon monoxide, hydrocarbon, and nitrogen oxide emissions. The first 2 years' efforts on setting standards for auto emissions progressed on schedule. But by the middle of 1973, the EPA began to encounter a series of problems. Mazmanian and Sabatier (1983, pp. 86-137) describe this as the beginning of an implementation period in which the EPA's strategy became unraveled. This unraveling occurred in response to "external pressure" from a number of lawsuits brought against the EPA, and as a consequence of the Arab oil embargo of that period.

In implementing the Clean Air Act, the EPA required states to include transportation control plans aimed at reducing reliance on the pollution-causing automobile. In 1972 the EPA granted a one-year extension to states for providing these plans; however, a number of environmental organizations filed suit against the EPA, and the federal courts agreed that the EPA had exceeded its authority in granting this extension. At the same time, the automobile industry requested a one-year extension of the emission standards for 1975-1976 models. The EPA rejected this request. As a result, a suit was filed by International Harvester, claiming that the technology at the time would not be able to meet the standards, and the federal court ordered the EPA to reconsider its decision. The EPA acquiesced and granted a one-year extension in 1973. Other law-suits challenged whether the EPA had the authority to require states to enforce state transportation plans prepared by the EPA. The court rulings created serious doubt about whether the EPA could impose sanctions on state and local governments.

When these events were combined with the Arab oil embargo of 1973, and the resulting massive increases in gasoline prices, enthusiasm for auto emission standards waned. Concern for improved air quality quickly changed to concern about improved fuel efficiency in cars. The efforts to improve the air, especially the pollution control equipment being placed in new cars, made gas efficiency suffer. Ultimately, the 1972 Act was not able to achieve its major goals, largely because of implemen-tation difficulties (Stewart, 1977); emissions reductions were not achieved because of missed deadlines; and reductions in the number of miles driven were not achieved because state transportation plans were not followed or enforced (Mazmanian & Sabatier, 1983, p. 117).

Implementing the 1977 Amendments

By late 1976 it became clear that the timetable envisioned in the 1970 Act was seriously flawed. As a consequence, in 1977 Congress enacted some amendments that tried to provide clearer and more realistic guid-ance. These Amendments extended the deadlines for the states to com-ply. The deadline for achieving the national ambient standards estab-lished by the EPA was extended to 1982, and in special circumstances to 1987. But beyond this, the Amendments added a somewhat less stringent technology requirement for polluters in heavily polluted air quality regions. This less stringent technology, called the "reasonably available control technology," sought to establish the "lowest emission limit that a particular source is capable of meeting by the application of control technology that is reasonably available considering techno-logical and economic feasibility." In other words, states would no longer have to impose the most expensive technological solution (com-pared to the "best available control technology" or technology to meet the "lowest achievable emission rate") on polluters within their respec-tive air quality regions. Instead, they could simply require the use of reasonable technologies.

As anticipated by the 1977 Amendments, the EPA and the states would apply this technology requirement to individual polluters on a case-by-case basis. In implementing these requirements, EPA and state agencies opted instead to develop guidelines and regulations specifying the reasonably available technology that would apply to entire industries. These blanket guidelines and regulations, in many cases, seemed to have eliminated some of the flexibility that Congress thought desirable to avoid creating economic hardship on specific polluting facilities and stifling economic development in entire regions.

Perhaps partly because the states' previous years of experience with the 1970 Act enabled them to be much more careful, and because EPA feared possible political backlash if broad sanctions were applied to states not complying, the EPA invented the idea of granting "conditional approval" to state implementation plans. Thus, even though a state's plan might have had serious flaws, the EPA could still approve the plan (achieving compliance with the law), and continue working with the state to remedy the flaws (Liroff, 1986, pp. 27-28). By 1981 the National Commission on Air Quality (1981, p. 117), an agency independent of the EPA, reported that the EPA had accepted virtually all of the states' implementation plans, even though there seemed to be widespread recognition that these plans were not going to lead to achievement of national ambient air quality standards. Perhaps even more disturbing, the Commission (1981, pp. 3.4-3.6) reported that by the end of 1980 there were some 489 counties that did not meet the national ambient standard for ozone, and there were 21 large metropolitan areas where the ozone standard was exceeded by at least 50%. Although compliance for other pollutants was better, there were still 40 counties that did not meet the ambient standard for carbon monoxide, and 18 counties that did not meet the sulfur dioxide standard.

This experience with implementing the 1977 Amendments provides a clear example of the clash between values of science and politics, as described in Chapter 1. Understanding the implementation process as involving such a clash helps to explain why many ambient air quality standards were not met. In typical clashes of these values, there are competing expectations about the role of scientific information and knowledge in policy-making. On one hand, based on the values of science, scientific and technological information is expected to dictate or guide major decisions. On the other hand, based on practical politics, scientific and technical information will simply be molded to support the politically desired action. The 1977 Amendments (and the 1970

Amendments as well) seemed to accept the assumption that the state implementation plans would be based solely on scientific and technical information and knowledge. The states would seek the most reliable and highest quality information, build this information into their plans, and then simply formulate implementation plans that fulfilled the letter and spirit of the law. But in practice, there is substantial reason to believe that these expectations were not borne out, and that state implementation plans were simply fashioned to support whatever action (or inaction) there was for political reasons.

It was not uncommon for states to rely very heavily on information directly from the polluters about amounts of specific emissions. Additionally, there was no single preferred or prescribed way (or model) of estimating how much specific pollutants would have to be reduced in given air quality regions. Even within the same state, state implementation plans frequently used whatever methods they deemed appropriate to make such estimates. For example, a report prepared by a consultant for the National Commission on Air Quality examined the methods that were used in the Ohio implementation plan to estimate how much each city would have to reduce various pollutants in order to meet the national ambient standards. This report suggested that Ohio officials could have used either one of two techniques to make their estimates. But neither technique was applied uniformly to all of the cities or air quality districts. Instead, each city used the technique that provided it with estimates requiring the least emission reductions. Consequently, Liroff (1986, p. 28) summarizes the futility of the science-over-politics set of expectations:

> These differences in abatement requirements, so dependent on the model used by [state] regulators, underscore the fictional nature of state implementation plans. As products of scientific uncertainty and administrative accommodation, assumptions and calculations may have only the most tenuous relationship to actual air quality and emissions, and projections of attainment may be worth little.

The 1977 Amendments sought to expedite the process of identifying and regulating "hazardous air pollutants," those pollutants that could cause serious and irreversible health effects. The 1977 law specified that the EPA was to identify such pollutants and issue regulations on their emissions within 6 months. Through the 1970s the EPA seemed to adopt the position that Congress did not intend for this requirement to be implemented very strictly because of potential economic harm. Consequently, the EPA seemed to prefer to avoid listing any pollutant as hazardous unless there was " almost irrefutable scientific evidence" that harm would occur (National Council on Air Quality, 1981, p. 77). By 1977 the EPA had identified and issued standards for only four hazardous air pollutants—asbestos, beryllium, mercury, and vinyl chloride. In the 1977 law, Congress expressed its dissatisfaction with the length of time EPA took to comply with this requirement, so it added four additional substances—arsenic, cadmium, radioactive contaminants, and polycyclic organic substances—for EPA to consider. Radioactive pollutants and arsenic were listed as hazardous by mid-1980. Additionally, by the end of 1980, the EPA listed and proposed emissions standards for sources of benzene pollution, with final standards to be in place by the beginning of 1982.

One might be left with the impression that, with all of these implementation problems, the federal efforts to clean up the air have been total failures. However, there is little question that between 1970 and 1980, significant reductions in air pollution were actually achieved. The Council on Environmental Quality (1981) reported that significant reductions in air pollution were evident, including 25% reductions in sulfur dioxide and 30% reductions in particulates. But there is considerable disagreement about whether the federal policy and its implementation caused these reductions. For example, MacAvoy (1979) has argued that changes in the design of cars, brought about by changes in the national economy and the rising price of gasoline, were largely responsible for reductions in auto emissions. On the other hand, White (1982, pp. 77-87) argues that "almost all of the actual reductions in emissions should be credited to the regulations themselves." There seems to be much less question of whether air pollution improved over this period.

Implementing Air Pollution Policy
in the Reagan Administration

As described previously, the 1980s ushered in an era in which air pollution policy implementation might be characterized as turbulent. The inauguration of President Reagan in 1981 signaled to many the time to roll back federal air pollution regulation. Many business interests, including the U.S. automobile industry, the U.S. Chamber of Commerce, and other industries, saw this as an opportunity to shed the economic burdens imposed on them by what they considered onerous federal regulatory requirements. When Reagan spoke of deregulation in order to get the federal government off their backs, these interests saw this as the time to get federal regulations off their backs.

The Clean Air Act Amendments became a clear target for this deregulatory zeal. A few weeks before Reagan's inauguration, David Stockman (who became Reagan's first director of the Office of Management and Budget) released a planning document on deregulation, in which half of the specific regulatory changes were directed at the clean air regulations (Tobin, 1984, p. 230). Shortly after Reagan's inauguration, Vice-President (later to become President) George Bush led a Task Force on Regulatory Relief, which issued some 18 recommendations to reduce the burden that clean air regulations created for the automobile industry. Included among these were strong requests to the EPA to reconsider its regulations seeking to eliminate lead additives from gasoline, and to revise, delay, or revoke regulations in other areas (Tobin, p. 236).

There were at least two ways this deregulatory zeal impacted federal clean air policy. First, as described earlier, the Reagan administration sought to get Congress to change the law. Failing this, the administration acted to accomplish through administrative implementation what it could not get through Congress. Perhaps the greatest impacts were on areas other than air pollution, but it seems clear that EPA administrators did their best to drag their feet in setting and enforcing standards. For example, Tobin (pp. 240-241) describes how the EPA's timetable for issuing standards for hazardous air pollutants came to a near standstill. Indeed, the EPA timetable under the Carter administration and the early Reagan administration called for standards to be in place by mid-1981 for radioactive pollutants and inorganic arsenic, and for final standards applying to benzene by early 1982. However, standards for the former were not proposed until 1983, after the federal courts mandated action, and final standards for benzene were still not in place at the beginning of 1984. In fact, the EPA withdrew proposed standards for benzene, noting that it no longer believed benzene from a number of sources posed a health threat. Similar experiences with missed deadlines, and the lack of apparent effort to meet them, characterized air pollution policy implementation with respect to new sources of air pollution, acid rain, and motor vehicle emissions as well.

Additionally, efforts were made to reverse some of the regulations already in place. For example, in 1982 the EPA revoked the standard for hydrocarbon pollution because it felt that hydrocarbons were not proven to produce adverse health effects. EPA also took actions designed to relax the phaseout of lead additives in gasoline. Human exposure to lead has repeatedly been found to cause serious health consequences, including severe neurological damage, mental retardation, and blindness, with the risks to children being extremely high, even at very low levels of exposure. Congress became so convinced that the EPA was more interested in the economic well-being of the petroleum industry than the physical health of people that it intervened, and ultimately the EPA, responding to congressional pressure, tightened rather than relaxed the lead regulations (Tobin, p. 237).

Even after the resolution of personnel and related issues at the EPA, the Reagan administration's posture toward air pollution policy implementation was not particularly aggressive. For example, the administration's position with respect to regulations directed toward acid rain was that no actions were warranted because the Clean Air Act Amendments did not *require* such action. Instead of taking initiative under existing legislation to implement programs that would affect acid rain and related problems, the administration declined to do so unless congressional action explicitly required it. At the same time, the administration also declined to put forth legislative initiatives to combat acid rain, instead preferring to call for more research (Regens & Rycroft, 1988, pp. 28-34).

The Evolution of the EPA's Air Pollution "Bubble" Policy

While all of the other debates and actions were taking place during the 1970s and 1980s, efforts to create a flexible yet effective air pollution policy began to shift to a "bubble" approach to regulating air emissions. This approach creates a mechanism for the trading of pollution credits, so that one polluter can benefit from cutting emissions below required standards, while another polluter can save money by purchasing these credits from the first. The bubble analogy stems from the idea of placing an imaginary bubble or dome over a group of air pollution sources, and suggests that a specific air quality standard would apply to emissions from the entire bubble rather than any single source within the bubble. The polluters under the bubble can adjust the amounts each contributes to achieve the most economical reduction of emissions. Economists have long advocated such approaches as ways of reducing pollution while minimizing the economic detriment.

Liroff suggests that the genesis of a federal bubble policy for air pollution occurred under the Carter administration during 1977 and

1978. Within EPA, the idea of a bubble policy took hold in the Office of Planning and Management. The use of bubbles was also advocated by a number of industries, including some that were chronic violators of air pollution standards. Indeed, one of the reasons why some in EPA apparently turned to a bubble approach was because they were looking for a way to get some of these industries, especially steel manufacturing, utilities, and smelters, to pollute less without creating undue financial burdens or without taking concerted legal action.

Bubbles were not advocated by everyone within EPA, and many environmental interest groups became quite concerned about its implications. Inside EPA, many officials in the air and enforcement divisions were less than enthusiastic about this concept, mainly because they felt that adoption of such a policy would send the wrong message to polluters who were looking for reasons not to comply with ambient standards. Environmental groups, especially the Natural Resources Defense Council, viewed the development of a bubble policy as evidence that the EPA was backing away from its own regulatory requirements. And many state officials, also believing that bubbles would undermine the progress they had made in reducing air emissions, expressed concern that such a policy would add another set of federal regulations requiring their compliance (Liroff, 1986, pp. 36-39).

The EPA continued work through the 1980s on developing a bubble policy. In mid-1978, the EPA established a task force to assess the feasibility of the bubble concept and recommend ways that it could be designed and implemented. The report of this task force, issued later that year, proved quite favorable to the idea while also pointing out some pitfalls. It recommended, for example, that under no circumstances should EPA allow trading within a bubble such that one polluter could reduce its nonhazardous emissions below existing standards, receive a credit, and then trade that credit to another polluter so that it could emit hazardous substances (Liroff, p. 40). In 1979 the EPA proposed its first bubble policy, which carried a number of fairly stringent conditions limiting the kinds of trades that could be made. Even so, the Natural Resources Defense Council, the Sierra Club Legal Defense Fund, and even a number of state air pollution control administrators expressed their opposition to this policy.

Despite opposition, the EPA issued a revised bubble policy in December 1979. Although this would seem to represent a political victory for advocates of the bubble approach, Liroff (pp. 46-47) suggests that the victory was largely symbolic because the policy was not accompanied by increased funding or staffing to implement it. It was not until mid-1982 that the EPA had developed its Emissions Trading Policy Statement, outlining how and when the policy could be applied to specific situations. Throughout the 1980s the EPA worked to refine the policy, sometimes expanding the conditions under which it could be used and making the requirements less stringent. Increasingly, states began to incorporate the use of bubbles for specific air quality regions, and the EPA settled on its final revised rules in 1986.

Specific Air Pollution-Related Problems

Up until now, this chapter has focused on federal legislation and its policy-making processes. Although various legislation has implications for specific types of air pollution and related problems, it is sometimes difficult to see what the policy toward a specific pollution problem is. Here the focus is on some of these problems. In particular, policies aimed at the problems of acid rain, the greenhouse effect, and thinning of the ozone layer of the atmosphere will be described more directly. Federal efforts to affect all of these problems may be found in a number of legislative and administrative actions. So now an effort will be made to answer the question: "What has been done to reduce acid rain, to reverse the greenhouse effect, to halt atmospheric ozone deterioration, to reduce the risks from exposure to radon gas, and to eliminate asbestos hazards?"

Public Policy Toward Acid Rain and the Greenhouse Effect

Over the past 10 years, efforts to pursue public policies to combat acid rain and global warming associated with the greenhouse effect have coalesced around efforts to fight specific types of air pollution (Lave, 1988). Largely because many of the same pollutants have been implicated in both sets of problems, efforts to address one also might be expected to affect the others. As noted in Chapter 1, each of these problems is thought to be caused by various types of sulfur and nitrogen oxide emissions. So public policies addressing both of these problems must be focused on reducing emissions of sulfur and nitrogen oxides.

The 1970 and 1977 Clean Air Act Amendments were not designed to address issues such as acid rain. The principal difficulty with taking federal action under authority of these laws was that both statutes assumed that actions against air pollution should primarily be a state and local responsibility. Implicit in this was the idea that states would be more aggressive if the problems created by air pollution were serious enough, and would not have to be so aggressive if air pollution were not a problem (Pederson, 1981). However, perhaps more than any other threat to the environment, the threat from acid rain points to the limitations of this concept. The air pollution that causes acid rain does not respect local and state geographic boundaries; the emissions from one state or region create problems for others. The state of Ohio, for example, has little incentive to take actions to limit acid rain-causing air emissions from coal-burning electric power plants because it does not have a serious problem with acid rain. Additionally, if the state did take actions, increasing the cost of producing electricity, the people of Ohio would have to pay. Thus, the issue of who pays and who benefits can act as a disincentive for action under the Clean Air Act Amendments. This is not to say that all states where acid rain-causing air pollution is generated have been against efforts to take action. As discussed shortly, a number of states have taken initiatives in this area.

Consistent with the notion that air pollution is primarily a state and local problem, the EPA instituted its State Acid Rain Program in 1985. This program was created under authority of the Clean Air Act, and supported technical, research, and management assistance by providing grants to individual states or groups of states. Although these grants did not support many direct actions aimed at reducing acid rain-causing air pollution, they apparently did help provide initial impetus for solving some technical problems that inevitably had to be addressed when a national acid rain policy was adopted (Regens & Rycroft, 1988, pp. 144-145).

Because the earlier federal legislation had already led to creation of national ambient air standards, many people, including those representing environmental groups and people who live in areas of the country most heavily affected by acid rain, argued that this provided a precedent for the federal EPA to impose standards on the states for the benefits of the nation as a whole, even if to do so would create local economic hardship. Others, however, such as members of the Bush administration and officials from midwestern electric utilities, have suggested that, under the earlier laws, the EPA could not impose such standards, especially if they would create local economic hardship. Thus, they argued that new federal legislation would be required to enable EPA action. The Reagan administration's position on acid rain through the 1980s was that existing legislation did not require them to take greater action, and that new legislation would not be sought until the scientific uncertainties perceived to be associated with acid rain were resolved (Regens & Rycroft, p. 32; USEPA, 1983).

The Bush administration took a similar position, again arguing that existing legislation was not adequate to combat either acid rain or the greenhouse effect. Unlike the Reagan administration, however, the Bush administration put forth legislative initiatives to provide the clear legal basis for EPA action. Congress provided this new legislation in the form of the 1990 Clean Air Act, described earlier. This Act was clearly focused by the Bush administration and Congress on the problems of acid rain and the greenhouse effect. Since the legislation is relatively recent, there is no implementation record to examine. However, the Act is fairly specific in how it anticipates the implementation to take place. As noted earlier, the Act seeks to reduce annual emissions of sulfur dioxide by some 10 million tons, representing about a 40% reduction from the 1980 pollution level of 25 tons. It seeks to do this while avoiding having these reductions canceled out by new emissions from new sources.

The 1990 Act calls for implementing reductions of sulfur and nitrogen oxide emissions in two incremental stages in order to phase in the added costs of compliance that might be passed on to consumers. The main target of the Act is electric power-generating facilities that burn coal and fossil fuel, especially high-sulfur coal. In the first stage, power plants that produce more than 100 megawatts of electricity are to reduce their annual emissions so that sulfur dioxide would not exceed 2.5 pounds for every million BTUs of heat produced. Greater reductions are called for in the second stage.

This Act targets polluters in specific areas of the country. Because most of the sulfur dioxide emitted into the air comes from electric utilities in the Midwest and the East, most of the limitations are focused there. Table 3.3 presents a list of the specific utilities targeted by this Act. Although there is only one source of pollution west of the Mississippi targeted in stage one, 107 plants in 20 eastern states are required to reduce emissions in the two stages, and about 700 plants throughout the country would be subject to new standards in stage two. Virtually none of the plants in the western part of the nation would be affected because they usually burn low-sulfur coal and already emit very little sulfur dioxide. The Act also places a limit on the total amount of sulfur dioxide emissions. This means that new sources of pollution are permitted only if the amount of pollution from these sources is offset by

Text continued on page 98

Table 3.3 Utilities Targeted for Special Reductions, and New Sulfur Dioxide Emissions Allowances, Under the Clean Air Act of 1990

Alabama		Coffeen-2	35,670
Colbert-1	13,570	Grand Tower-4	5,910
Colbert-2	15,310	Hennepin-2	18,410
Colbert-3	15,400	Joppa Steam-1	12,590
Colbert-4	15,410	Joppa Steam-2	10,770
Colbert-5	37,180	Joppa Steam-3	12,270
E. C. Gaston-1	18,100	Joppa Steam-4	11,360
E. C. Gaston-2	18,540	Joppa Steam-5	11,420
E. C. Gaston-3	18,310	Joppa Steam-6	10,620
E. C. Gaston-4	19,280	Kincaid-1	31,530
E. C. Gaston-5	59,840	Kincaid-2	33,810
Florida		Meredosia-3	13,890
Big Bend-1	28,410	Vermilion-2	8,880
Big Bend-2	27,100	Indiana	
Big Bend-3	26,740	Bailly-7	11,180
Crist-6	19,200	Bailly-8	15,630
Crist-7	31,680	Breed-1	18,500
Georgia		Cayuga-1	33,370
Bowen-1	56,320	Cayuga-2	34,130
Bowen-2	54,770	Clifty Creek-1	20,150
Bowen-3	71,750	Clifty Creek-2	19,810
Bowen-4	71,740	Clifty Creek-3	20,410
Hammond-1	8,780	Clifty Creek-4	20,080
Hammond-2	9,220	Clifty Creek-5	19,360
Hammond-3	8,910	Clifty Creek-6	20,380
Hammond-4	37,640	E. W. Stout-5	3,880
J. McDonough-1	19,910	E. W. Stout-6	4,770
J. McDonough-2	20,600	E. W. Stout-7	23,610
Wansley-1	70,770	F. B. Culley-2	4,290
Wansley-2	65,430	F. B. Culley-3	16,970
Yates-1	7,210	F. E. Ratts-1	8,330
Yates-2	7,040	F. E. Ratts-2	8,480
Yates-3	6,950	Gibson-1	40,400
Yates-4	8,910	Gibson-2	41,010
Yates-5	9,410	Gibson-3	41,080
Yates-6	24,760	Gibson-4	40,320
Yates-7	21,480	H. T. Pritchard-6	5,770
Illinois		Michigan City-12	23,310
Baldwin-1	42,010	Petersburg-1	16,430
Baldwin-2	44,420	Petersburg-2	32,380
Baldwin-3	42,550	R. Gallagher-1	6,490
Coffeen-1	11,790	R. Gallagher-2	7,280

continued

Table 3.3 Continued

R. Gallagher-3	6,530	Michigan	
R. Gallagher-4	7,650	J. H. Campbell-1	19,280
Tanners Creek-4	24,820	J. H. Campbell-2	23,060
Wabash River-1	4,000	Minnesota	
Wabash River-2	2,860	High Bridge-6	4,270
Wabash River-3	3,750	Mississippi	
Wabash River-5	3,670	Jack Watson-4	17,910
Wabash River-6	12,280	Jack Watson-5	36,700
Warrick-4	26,980	Missouri	
Iowa		Asbury-1	16,190
Burlington-1	10,710	James River-55	4,850
Des Moines-7	2,320	Labadie-1	40,110
George Neal-1	1,290	Labadie-2	37,710
M. L. Kapp-2	13,800	Labadie-3	40,310
Prairie Creek-4	8,180	Labadie-4	35,940
Riverside-5	3,990	Montrose-1	7,390
Kansas		Montrose-2	8,200
Quindaro-2	4,220	Montrose-3	10,090
Kentucky		New Madrid-1	28,240
Coleman-1	1,125	New Madrid-2	32,490
Coleman-2	12,840	Sibley-3	15,580
Coleman-3	12,340	Sioux-1	22,570
Cooper-1	7,450	Sioux-2	23,690
Cooper-2	15,320	Thomas Hill-11	10,250
E. W. Brown-1	7,110	Thomas Hill-2	19,390
E. W. Brown-2	10,910	New Hampshire	
E. W. Brown-3	26,100	Merrimack-1	10,190
Elmer Smith-1	6,520	Merrimack-2	22,000
Elmer Smith-2	14,410	New Jersey	
Ghent-1	28,410	B. L. England-1	9,060
Green River-4	7,820	B. L. England-2	11,720
H. L. Spurlock-1	22,780	New York	
Henderson II-1	13,340	Dunkirk-3	12,600
Henderson II-2	12,310	Dunkirk-4	14,060
Paradise-3	59,170	Greenidge-4	7,540
Shawnee-10	10,170	Milliken-1	11,170
Maryland		Milliken-2	12,410
Chalk Point-1	21,890	Northport-1	19,810
Chalk Point-2	24,330	Northport-2	24,110
C. P. Crane-1	10,330	Northport-3	26,480
C. P. Crane-2	9,230	Port Jefferson-3	10,470
Morgantown-1	35,260	Port Jefferson-4	12,330
Morgantown-2	38,480		

continued

Table 3.3 Continued

Ohio		Pennsylvania	
Ashtabula-5	16,740	Armstrong-1	14,410
Avon Lake-8	11,650	Armstrong-2	15,430
Avon Lake-9	30,480	Brunner Island-1	27,760
Cardinal-1	34,270	Brunner Island-2	31,100
Cardinal-2	38,320	Brunner Island-3	53,820
Conesville-1	4,210	Cheswick-1	39,170
Conesville-2	4,890	Conemaugh-1	59,790
Conesville-3	5,500	Conemaugh-2	66,450
Conesville-4	48,770	Hatfield's Ferry-1	37,830
Eastlake-1	7,800	Hatfield's Ferry-2	37,320
Eastlake-2	8,640	Hatfield's Ferry-3	40,270
Eastlake-3	10,020	Martins Creek-1	12,660
Eastlake-4	14,510	Martins Creek-2	12,820
Eastlake-5	34,070	Portland-1	5,940
Edgewater-4	5,050	Portland-2	10,230
Gen. J. M. Gavin-1	79,080	Shawville-1	10,320
Gen. J. M. Gavin-2	80,560	Shawville-2	10,320
Kyger Creek-1	19,280	Shawville-3	14,220
Kyger Creek-2	18,560	Shawville-4	14,070
Kyger Creek-3	17,910	Sunbury-3	8,760
Kyger Creek-4	18,710	Sunbury-4	11,450
Kyger Creek-5	18,740	Tennessee	
Miami Fort-5	760	Allen-1	15,320
Miami Fort-6	11,380	Allen-2	16,770
Miami Fort-7	38,510	Allen-3	15,670
Muskingum River-1	14,880	Cumberland-1	86,700
Muskingum River-2	14,170	Cumberland-2	94,840
Muskingum River-3	13,950	Gallatin-1	17,870
Muskingum River-4	11,780	Gallatin-2	17,310
Muskingum River-5	40,470	Gallatin-3	20,020
Niles-1	6,940	Gallatin-4	21,260
Niles-2	9,100	Johnsonville-1	7,790
Picway-5	4,930	Johnsonville-2	8,040
R. E. Burger-3	6,150	Johnsonville-3	8,410
R. E. Burger-4	10,780	Johnsonville-4	7,990
R. E. Burger-5	12,430	Johnsonville-5	8,240
W. H. Sammis-5	24,170	Johnsonville-6	7,890
W. H. Sammis-6	39,930	Johnsonville-7	8,980
W. H. Sammis-7	43,220	Johnsonville-8	8,700
W. C. Beckjord-5	8,950	Johnsonville-9	7,080
W. C. Beckjord-6	23,020	Johnsonville-10	7,550

continued

Table 3.3 Continued

West Virginia		Wisconsin	
Albright-3	12,000	Edgewater-4	24,750
Fort Martin-1	41,590	La Crosse Genoa-3	22,700
Fort Martin-2	41,200	Nelson Dewey-1	6,010
Harrison-1	48,620	Nelson Dewey-2	6,680
Harrison-2	46,150	N. Oak Creek-1	5,220
Harrison-3	41,500	N. Oak Creek-2	5,140
Kammer-1	18,740	N. Oak Creek-3	5,370
Kammer-2	19,460	N. Oak Creek-4	6,320
Kammer-3	17,390	Pulliam-8	7,510
Mitchell-1	43,980	S. Oak Creek-5	9,670
Mitchell-2	45,510	S. Oak Creek-6	12,040
Mount Storm-1	43,720	S. Oak Creek-7	16,180
Mount Storm-2	35,580	S. Oak Creek-8	15,790
Mount Storm-3	42,430		

SOURCE: P.L. 404(e) Table A

reductions from existing sources. Allowing this law to be implemented in a flexible way, the Act also calls for pollution credits and trading very much consistent with the EPA's bubble policy.

Although the vast majority of acid rain attention has focused on federal policies, since about 1984 a number of states have taken initiative to curb air pollution thought to cause acid rain and the greenhouse effect. For example, the state of New York adopted its Acid Rain Deposition Control Act of 1984, which called for the development of a specific plan to deal with acid rain. Other states, such as New Hampshire and Wisconsin, also took specific actions. The state of Michigan actually negotiated its own international agreement with Ontario, Canada, calling for the sharing of air emissions information and research (Regens & Rycroft, pp. 141-145). However, even these efforts have not escaped the problems created by the distribution of costs and benefits across states. For example, in an effort to protect miners in its high-sulfur coal mines, the Indiana legislature approved a 1984 resolution calling for Congress to target northeastern states for control (Regens & Rycroft, p. 143).

Public Policy Toward Ozone Depletion

The problem of depletion of atmospheric ozone has not received quite as much attention in public policy as have other air pollution problems, perhaps because acid rain and the greenhouse effect appear to have more immediate health and environmental effects. Just as there has been little agreement on whether the ozone layer of the atmosphere has actually been affected by air pollution, there has been little agreement on whether the federal government or governments of other nations ought to take public policy action. Until very recently, the federal government has focused largely on ozone depletion within an international context, pursuing voluntary means of seeking long-term reductions in the use of chemicals that act to deplete atmospheric ozone.

As early as 1974 the United States, Canada, Norway, and Sweden took actions to ban CFCs as propellants in aerosol cans. Member countries of the European Community agreed in 1980 not to increase the use of CFCs, and to reduce their use in aerosol cans by 30% by 1982. Perhaps the single largest step in the international community to curb the manufacture and use of CFCs was the result of the "Montreal Protocol." In 1987 representatives from the governments of many industrialized nations met in Montreal to begin working on a pact that would seek to phase out CFCs and replace them with less environmentally damaging alternatives. The agreement called for production of CFCs to be frozen at 1986 levels by 1989; a 20% decrease in production of CFCs by 1993; another 30% reduction by 1998; and a freeze on halon production at 1986 levels by 1992.

For this pact to take effect, at least 11 nations would have to ratify it, and the ratifying nations would have to account for two-thirds of the international consumption of CFCs. Although the ratification of this agreement met the requirements, the agreement itself has been criticized for containing many "loopholes" that permit nations to avoid complying. The agreement has provisions that allow deadlines to be extended for specific nations, and many of the definitions used in the agreement are subject to interpretation (Shea, 1988, pp. 32-33). Each ratifying nation would be permitted to achieve specified reductions in its own way. However, it is clear that there is some variation in the amount of domestic support for compliance. While Sweden apparently has taken the position that the development of less harmful replacements provides an immense business opportunity, the United States, Japan, and Germany have expressed considerable concern that compliance would affect economic competitiveness. None of these nations seems terribly enthusiastic about taking actions by itself because of fear of becoming less competitive in the world marketplace (Shea, pp. 31-32).

Additionally, since the Protocol was signed, many scientific estimates have raised serious questions about whether full compliance would be enough to save the ozone layer. For example, the EPA has estimated that under the Protocol, even with every nation of the world complying, chlorine gas concentrations in the atmosphere will more than triple (Shea, 1988, p. 33). And many chemicals that apparently contribute to ozone depletion, such as methyl chloroform and carbon tetrachloride, are not covered by the Protocol. Consequently, increased use of these chemicals, permitted under the Protocol, would contribute to continued ozone depletion.

In the United States, early efforts focused on voluntary industrial actions to limit production and use of ozone-depleting chemicals. One such effort has concentrated on the automobile manufacture and repair industries. It has been estimated that perhaps as much as one-third of one type of CFC used in air-conditioners is emitted into the air through leakage, and much of that comes from leaking car air-conditioners. The air-conditioning industry has developed voluntary standards on how freon from car air-conditioners should be recovered and recycled. The EPA has suggested that if the auto servicing industry does not comply by 1992, it may issue regulations to make recovery and recycling practices mandatory.

In 1990, with the enactment of the Clean Air Act, Congress took explicit action with respect to ozone depletion. In addition to the benefits to atmospheric ozone that would accrue from other provisions, this legislation specifically called for a total phaseout of major ozone-depleting CFCs. It provides a clear timetable for the phaseout of both use and production of chemicals known to have ozone-depleting capabilities, giving priority to those chemicals with the greatest ozone-depleting potential, with full phaseout to be completed by the year 2000. The timetable, if followed, would far exceed the requirements of the Montreal Protocol.

A Summary of Air Pollution Policy Controversies

This chapter discussed many different controversies, contemporary and historical, surrounding air pollution policy in the United States. The controversies have involved issues of the proper role of government in protecting and improving the quality of air, and the role of the federal versus state governments in setting and enforcing air quality standards. The governmental role in air pollution control started very modestly, perhaps yielding to the belief that governmental involvement was limited. As air pollution was perceived as becoming worse, and as federal officials increasingly perceived that reliance on the states was not a very effective way to pursue cleaner air, the federal role grew. With the recognition that state and local governments might not have the incentive or resources to take actions against some types of pollution, such as those contributing to acid rain, the role of the federal government has grown.

Expanded federal involvement in air pollution policy occurred with the passage of the Clean Air Act Amendments of 1970, which were enacted by Congress in response to "policy escalation," where a number of distinctly different actors in the policy-making process competed with each other to come across as stronger advocates of environmental protection. The result was a piece of legislation that sought to achieve pollution abatement and control in ways not then feasible. This approach to air pollution control, referred to by Charles O. Jones as "speculative augmentation," does not seem to have produced better quality air as much as it created confusion, indecision, and sometimes conflict that had to be resolved by the courts.

Controversies have also arisen over how administrative agencies decided to interpret and implement various statutes. Air pollution legislation has placed a great deal of authority and discretion in the hands of federal agencies, especially the EPA. Consequently, the EPA has often been in the middle of intense political disagreements. Nowhere was this more evident than in the EPA during the first 3 years of the Reagan administration. Seemingly captured by the interests it was charged with regulating, the EPA came under fire from Congress and environmental groups for being less rather than more aggressive in fighting air pollution.

There have also been controversies concerning whether air pollution improvements should be sought even when short-term economic impacts appear to be substantial. In seeking a flexible policy that would achieve air quality improvements without causing economic hardship, EPA appeared to many to become soft on pollution. As the EPA pursued a bubble policy for pollution regulation, opponents read this as acquiescence to polluting industries that did not want to comply with the law.

Despite evidence of improvements in air quality, there remains substantial disagreement over whether federal air pollution policy has been responsible for these improvements. Skeptics suggest that market mechanisms and the lack of economic growth are largely responsible for air quality improvements, arguing that the quality of the air would have improved even without federal action. Others obviously believe that federal air pollution policy has had the desired effect, although not always to the extent desired. Passage of the 1990 Clean Air Act, for example, clearly assumes that additional federal and state controls on sulfur and nitrogen oxide emissions will reduce acid rain and possibly the greenhouse effect.

Not all of this country's air pollution problems or policies have been discussed in this chapter. There are many types of air pollution or sources of air pollution, especially those associated with the workplace, that have not been explicitly discussed. Efforts to affect air pollution from cattle, from dry cleaners, from aircraft, and many other sources have not been addressed here. Pollution in major urban areas, especially from automobiles, has not been discussed in great depth, although most of the discussion about air pollution standards has obvious implications for urban air pollution. Space constraints prevent a discussion of problems of radon gas, especially in private residences, and of asbestos, especially efforts to mandate asbestos removal from schools. There was very modest discussion of the sometimes innovative efforts made by state and local governments to improve the quality of their air, above and beyond what may be required by federal regulations. Some states, especially those with the worst problems, are beginning to take serious steps to curb their pollution.

The issues and problems that were discussed, however, provide a firm foundation for understanding some of the major controversies that persist in debates about public air pollution policy. Many of these same issues are likely to recur in future debates, even debates surrounding specific issues that are not yet recognized as problems. The problems may change, but many of the underlying clashes of values remain the same.

4

Public Policies to Protect and Improve the Quality of the Nation's Water

Although the federal government has had fairly lengthy experiences with trying to establish public policies that would protect and improve the quality of water supplies, the effort has been plagued by the need to balance a variety of goals. In early federal involvement in water policy, the federal government played the part of a weak partner, providing some money and technical assistance to state and local governments if they wanted it. The federal role was defined by an assumed prerogative of the states and localities to decide whether to tolerate or permit water pollution and water usage.

This began to change in the early 1970s, when Congress provided the legal authority for federal agencies to intervene on behalf of water pollution control. Yet the federal involvement did not always produce cleaner water, and certainly did not make many people happier with either the quality of or the access to water. Perhaps more than in any other environmental area, water pollution, protection, and preservation policy challenges the idea that there can be a single national policy that will work everywhere. As Tolley, Graves, and Blomquist (1981) have argued, "environmental policy should let the shoe fit, rather than insisting everyone wear the same size shoe" (p. 194).

AUTHOR'S NOTE: This chapter was written with the assistance of Denise Turgeon.

These words are especially applicable to water policy—its formulation, adoption, and implementation—in the United States. Since the early 1970s, high expectations and sweeping appropriations and regulations often have failed to take unique situations into account; policy-makers sometimes have set unreasonable or unattainable goals; and conflicts over money, especially who pays, have played a major part in water policy controversies. These issues are often masked by debate about which level of government—federal, state, or local—ought to exercise primary responsibility for water protection and improvement.

These specific issues and some of the broader issues referred to in Chapter 1 will be addressed. There are some issues related to public policies toward water not addressed, or at least not addressed in much depth, in this chapter. For example, one of the largest threats to America's water supplies relates to problems of toxic and hazardous waste disposal. However, this issue is addressed in Chapter 5. The issue of access to scarce water supplies, especially in arid regions of the United States, is discussed only very briefly. Public policies toward water pollution created by air pollution, such as acid rain, were discussed in Chapter 3. In this chapter, the focus is on federal and state regulation of effluent water discharges, efforts to protect wetland areas, regulatory activities to set standards for safe drinking water, and a host of political issues related to these efforts. The reasons for this central focus emerge from a brief review of the history of water policies in America since the mid-1950s, and the federal and state programs that make up these policies. This review also provides a useful foundation to understanding the current state of the nation's water policy.

Federal Water Legislation:
A Brief History Since 1956

There had been several, albeit infrequent, efforts by Congress before the 1950s to limit water pollution. For example, the Oil Pollution Act of 1924 sought to prohibit ocean vessels from routinely dumping oil in coastal waterways. Subsequently, the Water Pollution Control Act of 1948 started the federal government on a long path in water pollution control efforts (Davies & Davies, 1975, p. 27). This Act marked the start of a tradition defining the federal role in water policy as one limited to providing technical and financial assistance. The federal government

Table 4.1 Key Federal Water Pollution and Protection Legislation Since 1956

The Federal Water Pollution Control Act of 1956

The Clean Water Restoration Act of 1966

The Marine Resources and Engineering Development Act of 1966

The Water Quality Improvement Act of 1970

The Federal Water Pollution Control Act Amendments
   (Also known as the Clean Water Act) of 1972

The Marine Protection Research and Sanctuaries Act of 1972

The Coastal Zone Management Act of 1972

The Safe Drinking Water Act of 1974

The Coastal Zone Management Act Amendments of 1976

The Federal Water Pollution Control Act Amendments
   (Also known as The Clean Water Act) of 1977

The Coastal Zone Management Act Amendments of 1980

The Municipal Wastewater Treatment Construction Grant Amendments
   (Also known as The Clean Water Act Amendments) of 1981

Marine Protection, Research and Sanctuaries Reauthorization Act of 1981

The Safe Drinking Water Amendments and Reauthorization Act of 1986

The Coastal Zone Management Act Amendments of 1986

The Clean Water Act Amendments of 1987

The Safe Drinking Water Act Amendments of 1988

made its involvement in water regulation permanent in 1956, with the passage of the Federal Water Pollution Control Act (FWPCA). Since that time, Congress has enacted many laws designed to affect the quality of water. Table 4.1 provides a list of the major federal water policy legislation since 1956.

The FWPCA established a 5-year program allocating grants to municipalities to construct sewage treatment plant facilities. It provided $50 million each year and instituted enforcement procedures for interstate pollution control and technical assistance for state and regional water agencies. This Act, which was amended four times between 1961 and 1970, ultimately developed the first federal water quality standards program (Lieber, 1975, p. 21). Efforts by the agency then responsible for federal water policy implementation, the Federal Water Quality Control Administration, were very controversial, largely because of disputes with the states.

The next major piece of federal water legislation, the Clean Water Restoration Act of 1966, provided grants for the development of pollution control and abatement plans for river basins, a national esturine pollution study, and a study of how much it would cost industry to engage in pollution control. These grants allocated up to 50% of the administrative costs of these planning and research projects. This Act, its predecessors, and some of its successors, embraced a philosophy about the federal role in water pollution and protection that critics have pointed to as being fundamentally flawed. Such critics maintain that too much of the money appropriated was spent on salaries, studies, and administrative costs, rather than on construction of actual facilities or on abatement and pollution control activities.

As embraced by the Clean Water Restoration Act, the federal role in water pollution policy started out being limited to one of providing assistance to the states, with little effort to persuade or entice state and local governments to take water pollution control seriously. Although this philosophy began changing in the 1970s, one can still see vestiges of it in more contemporary federal water policy, as reflected in emphasis on conducting research, planning, and paying for administrative costs rather than actually mandating improved water quality. For example, in more recent times, this can be seen in the budget of EPA. From fiscal year 1981 to fiscal year 1983, a period of general retrenchment of the federal government from environmental policy, the EPA budget revealed that total allocations for salaries fell only about 2.3%, while the Clean Lakes Program, designed to fund actual cleanups of lakes, lost 72% of its funding, and abatement and pollution control activities lost 31% (Ledbetter, 1984, p. 52). The reemergence of the earlier philosophy in the EPA's budget may not have extended much beyond 1983, but it suggests that preference for limiting the federal role to one of assistance to the states is alive and well.

The passage of the Water Quality Improvement Act in 1970 provided for oil pollution controls. It allowed the federal government to take immediate action following oil spills, with the costs transferred to any party found to be at fault. Much of the federal role in oil spill events of the past several years, including the Exxon *Valdez* accident in Alaska's Prince William Sound, was based in large part on this piece of legislation. Some have suggested that such oil spills reveal the limitations of the federal government in taking directed action, and that these policies could be made more stringent. Although one could maintain that these spills are truly unfortunate but unavoidable accidents, some have argued that the penalties for such spills should become more severe. This argument suggests that if the penalties were made stiffer, several beneficial consequences would result: The executives of major oil companies would be less willing to take chances, less able to simply incorporate the costs of spills into the costs of doing business; presumably the captains of oil tankers such as the *Valdez* might be more careful in their duties; and oil companies might be more diligent in their hiring practices and procedures.

The philosophy of the proper role for the federal government in water quality and pollution control experienced a notable change in the early 1970s. Paralleling the changes in philosophy exhibited in air pollution control, the federal government started taking increased water policy responsibility in 1972, with the passage of the Federal Water Pollution Control Act Amendments (also referred to as the Clean Water Act of 1972). The title of this Act implies incremental changes from its 1956 counterpart, but the Act actually introduced a new era in federal water policy. This piece of legislation provided clear federal authority and responsibility for controlling water pollution through issuing permits, setting minimum clean water standards, and many other mechanisms. This ushered in what Crotty (1987) refers to as environmental "primacy policy," where the states are supposed to serve more as extensions of federal agencies for water pollution control implementation than as independent policy formulators and implementors in their own right. In a sense, this primacy policy appears to some to provide federal preemption of local water policy authority.

These Federal Water Pollution Control Act Amendments (the Clean Water Act) of 1972 expanded the 1956 FWPCA by increasing appropriations for construction grants to municipalities—$4.5 billion per year through 1975, compared with the $50 million provided under the FWPCA. More significantly, though, the Act set some specific goals for the nation's water cleanup program. This Act marked the first time that the federal government established national goals that would be applied and presumably enforced uniformly, although this would be done through state programs. According to Lieber (1975, pp. 10-11), this Act ushered in the first federal effort to directly regulate the quality of water. Some of the specified goals were directed toward the treatment of raw sewage. This Act also shifted regulatory attention from maintaining general water quality standards to establishing and enforcing effluent discharge standards. In other words, the focus of federal and state regulatory efforts shifted to specific polluters, rather than just trying to maintain the cleanliness of a particular body of water. In this way, polluters could be held accountable for the actual contamination they caused, and efforts could be made to stop water pollution at its source.

The cornerstone of the Clean Water Act that effectively accomplished this shift has been the National Pollutant Discharge Elimination System (NPDES). This system prohibits the discharge of any wastes or effluents by any industrial and governmental parties unless there is an explicit permit issued by a specific government agency. The permits specify how much, what kinds of, and over what time period pollutants can be discharged. Parties involved in the discharge of concentrated streams of environmentally damaging materials are required to apply for permits, specifying the limits of allowable pollution discharge and the appropriate measures to be taken to be sure the discharged materials meet the specified limits. The permits usually specify the *technological methods* that would be used to meet the standards.

The EPA has primary authority for issuing such permits, but it is allowed to delegate this authority to the states. States can make application to the EPA so that they can exercise authority over issuing and enforcing permits. The EPA developed guidelines for what information has to be contained in such applications. This includes, among other things, that a single agency in any given state perform the permitting function. Currently, all states have been delegated such authority, although some of the states that have most recently been delegated some authority exercise responsibility for only partial programs (Jessup, 1988, p. 7). Thus, all the states have gotten involved in water pollution regulation, limiting and attempting to control the nature of industrial and municipal wastewater and pollution discharges. Once a state's application has been approved by EPA, the EPA ceases to issue permits in that state. EPA usually retains jurisdiction over permits it issued prior to approval of a state's permit system.

Municipal wastewater treatment facilities are also subject to the NPDES requirements: Local sewage treatment plants cannot discharge wastes unless they have permits to do so. More than 21,000 municipal sewage treatment facilities became the targets of federal regulation (Rosenbaum, 1977, p. 159). Three levels of waste treatment were delineated, with the intent to produce cleaner and cleaner water by screening or filtering out contaminants. The first level, primary treatment or pretreatment, consists of passing wastewater through filters and screens, usually in an effort to mechanically remove pollutants and suspended matter. The second level, secondary treatment, requires more complex "trickling filters" or "activated sludge processes" to remove soluble organic wastes and suspended solids. The third level, advanced wastewater treatment, involves even more sophisticated chemical treatments, filtration devices, and biological processes. The process of treatment yields solid matter often referred to as "sludge," which contains increasingly concentrated amounts of pollutants that have been separated from clean water.

The FWPCA set July 1, 1977, as the deadline for the secondary treatment of all wastewater before eventually being discharged into other bodies of water (lakes, streams, and so on). By 1974 only about 3,400 municipal treatment facilities were able to meet the federal standards (Rosenbaum, 1977, p. 159). And despite the laudable goal set for 1977, only about one-third of all municipalities met this requirement by then, so Congress extended the deadline to 1983. According to the 1972 Amendments, municipal sewage discharged into waterways would no longer be allowed to receive any discharge of untreated pollutants.

This Act, along with its 1977 Amendments, required that polluters subject their effluent discharges to primary or pretreatment before discharging them. The issue of whether pretreatment should be made mandatory has become the focus of some controversy. The reason for requiring pretreatment is simply that most municipal sewage treatment facilities cannot cope with many chemical contaminants. Such facilities were frequently designed to handle only normal household wastes. Yet increasingly, municipal facilities found industrial contaminants among the waste streams with which they had to deal. The controversy arises out of an apparent lack of clear evidence that pretreatment makes municipal treatment easier or more effective. According to some, especially the business community, regulations requiring pretreatment would end up costing industry huge amounts of money to comply in the face of a lack of demonstrated need or definitive results (Mosher, 1982).

The 1972 Act also set an interim goal for the protection of aquatic life and wildlife, and resumption of recreation by 1983 (fishing, swimming, and boating) on all waterways where such activities had ceased because of pollution. Paralleling the ideas found in air pollution control legislation enacted about the same time, all concentrated "point" sources of water pollution discharge were to be reduced to "acceptable levels," using the "best practicable technology" by 1977 and the "best available technology" by 1983. It specified that there should be "zero discharge" of pollution by 1985. Point sources of pollution consist of specific concentrated and identifiable places where pollutants enter waterways, such as specific manufacturing industries, municipal sewage treatment plants, and so on. Under this Act, municipal sewage treatment plants were subjected to the less stringent standard of having to use the "best practicable" technology by 1983. The Act did very little to address pollution not from point sources, for reasons that will be described later.

The year 1972 also saw the Coastal Zone Management Act, the first major entry of the federal government into management and protection of coastal waters. Coastal zones were defined as the non-federal coastal waters and non-federal shorelands, including salt marshes, wetlands, and beaches. This Act provided federal grants to states that voluntarily prepared and implemented their own coastal zone management programs. As a matter of national policy, this Act sought to preserve, protect, and, where possible, restore or enhance coastal areas. In essence, this Act sought in part to influence the states to begin examining and presumably limiting coastal environmental damage produced by various kinds of economic development. It did not impose federal standards on state or local governments. Federal goals and standards evolved through the 1976, 1980, and 1986 Amendments to this Act. Unlike other environmental programs and policies, coastal zone management became the responsibility of the National Oceanic and Atmospheric Agency in the Commerce Department (Zile, 1974).

In 1974 Congress passed the Safe Drinking Water Act in an effort to protect underground sources of drinking water from potential contamination. Unlike earlier water quality legislation, this Act authorized the EPA to set uniform national standards for various specific pollution agents and required routine monitoring to check levels of the contaminants. At that time, more than 200 natural and synthetic substances had been detected in groundwater, but up until the mid-1980s, the EPA had established only 22 mandatory water quality standards covering only 18 specific chemicals (Foegen, 1986, p. 23). Noting that as much as 20% of the nation's population relies on private wells for drinking water, many critics urged the EPA to speed up issuance of regulations under the Safe Drinking Water Act. The 1986 Safe Drinking Water Reauthorization Act, as will be discussed shortly, calls for additional efforts in defining new chemical standards.

For the most part, the 1977 Amendments to the Federal Water Pollution Control Act simply changed the dates by which polluting parties must comply with the use of different technologies. As Meier (1985, p. 157) states:

Industries basically lobbied for relaxation of the 1972 standards, arguing that they were impossible to meet and that the 1985 "zero-discharge" goal could never be met. Congress responded to these interests. [Polluters] that acted in "good faith" to meet the 1977 policy of best practicable technology but failed to do so were given until 1979 to meet [this standard]. The 1983 best available technology goal was weakened to best conventional pollution control technology and was effective for 1984. Although the "zero-discharge" goal remained in the legislation, the 1977 amendments placed its attainment far into the future.

These 1977 Amendments also specified a heightened emphasis on regulating the discharge of toxic chemicals. Some reflections of this emphasis will be examined as part of hazardous waste policy, as discussed in Chapter 5.

The role of the federal government in financing water pollution control through facility grants remained fairly stable until the early 1980s. Indeed, while the role of the federal government in water policy remained substantial, the early 1980s witnessed the start of something of a shift in the philosophy governing this federal role. Paralleling efforts by the Reagan administration to devolve a range of policy responsibility to the states and away from the federal government, federal policies and programs began easing enforcement of water quality standards and rule-making. At the same time that greater responsibility was being left to state and local governments, federal financial contributions to state and local water pollution control efforts also began to shrink substantially.

While the 1977 Federal Water Pollution Control Act Amendments made some changes in the grant programs, for the most part they simply changed levels of funding or extended deadlines and expiration dates of grants. However, a major change came about in 1981, with the passage of the Municipal Wastewater Treatment Construction Grant Amendments (sometimes referred to as the Clean Water Act Amendments of 1981). This Act marked a period in which the Reagan administration and Congress sought to reduce the role of the federal government in financing state and local water treatment facilities. This legislation reauthorized the construction grant program through fiscal year 1985, but its allocations of $2.4 billion over 4 years would reduce the federal role in financing these facilities from a high of about 75% to only about 55%.

In addition to limiting federal funding of sewage treatment plant construction, the 1981 Act also reduced support for local interceptors, infiltration, and inflow correction projects. It exempted many ocean-discharging municipalities from the secondary treatment requirements, then allowing municipalities to avoid paying the costs of reducing pollution emissions. Up until 1981 the federal government provided funds to help municipalities create a 20-year reserve capacity, so that they would be prepared to handle increased future wastewater processing demands. The 1981 Act also limited federal funding for municipal treatment plant reserve capacity, beginning in 1985.

In June 1986 Congress enacted and President Reagan signed the amendments to and reauthorization of the Safe Drinking Water Act, reflecting a continuation of the basic philosophy underlying the federal role in water pollution policy while strengthening the actual implementation of that policy (Ketchum-Colwell, 1986). These amendments called for EPA to establish maximum contaminant level (MCL) goals, defined as levels of contamination that would cause no adverse health effects and would allow an adequate margin of safety. EPA was to set standards as close to these goals as was feasible, taking costs into consideration (CQWR, 1986, pp. 1126-1127). It required the EPA to set standards for allowable levels of chemicals in drinking water at a faster pace, specifying that by 1989, 83 specific chemicals, which had already been earmarked as candidates for regulation, were to have definite regulations. By 1988 EPA was required to develop a priority list of other contaminants for which standards were needed. States were to be stimulated to protect groundwater serving as the source for public (municipal) water, especially protecting public water supplies from hazardous waste sites and leaking landfills, pesticide runoff largely in agricultural areas, and leaking underground gas storage tanks. Public water systems were to use the "best available technology" to remove contamination, and to monitor for the presence of chemicals not already regulated.

Congress adopted another set of Clean Water Act Amendments in 1987. These amendments were designed to provide some mid-course corrections to water pollution policy and, in many ways, represented something of a small step backward from water pollution policy, by placing some new reporting requirements on the states, and providing the EPA with legal authority to apply less strict standards under some circumstances. The Amendments required the states to identify and communicate to the EPA a list of waterways that were expected to violate water quality standards because of the presence of toxic wastes, even after all point source dischargers of water pollution had installed the best available technology to reduce pollution discharges. Then states were required to identify the parties or sources responsible for discharging these toxic wastes, and design plants to control future discharges. The 1987 Amendments also included a provision which allowed the EPA to modify and make less stringent the limitations on polluters if the lower limitations were shown to cause economic hardship, as long as the polluter demonstrated that there had been progress toward reducing emissions in the recent past (Jessup, 1988, p. 11).

Protecting Wetlands:
Fragmented Policy, Difficult Implementation

Protection of the nation's wetlands has slowly but surely become a goal of federal water policy. It is estimated that the United States currently has less than half of the 215 million acres of wetlands present at the time of European settlement, and this figure does not include Alaska's acreage, which accounts for 60% of the state's area. Federal policy toward America's wetlands tends to be a little more complicated than that toward drinking water, sewage treatment, and other areas. It is more complicated for two major reasons. First, there is a much wider range of federal legislation that affects wetlands. A section of the 1972 Clean Water Act deals with the protection of the nation's wetlands, although most of the federal effort on wetlands protection has come through the Coastal Zone Management Act of 1972 and its 1976, 1980, and 1986 Amendments. And second, there are many federal and state agencies with overlapping interest in and jurisdiction over the wetlands. While the EPA exercises jurisdiction over some types of wetlands, much of the Coastal Zone legislation is the responsibility of the National Oceanic and Atmospheric Administration in the Commerce Department. Additionally, the U.S. Army Corps of Engineers has exercised authority over the nation's navigable waterways since about 1899, when Congress enacted the River and Harbors Act (sometimes referred to as the Refuse Act of 1899) (Jessup, 1988, p. 12). Some implications of this shared jurisdiction will be described shortly.

The loss of wetlands has occurred for many reasons, not the least of which is that for decades wetlands were considered prime areas for commercial and economic development. At best, existing federal laws only slow down the rate of loss. Despite an increasing awareness of the critical role that wetlands play in the world's delicate ecosystem, and evidence of increasing public support for wetlands protection, more concerted federal efforts in wetland protection face serious obstacles. Private conservation groups have increasingly organized efforts to purchase wetlands so that they can protect them, but the purchase of these lands is quite costly. Government efforts to acquire and protect wetlands probably always have been and always will be limited by budgetary pressures. Governments have occasionally tried enacting incentive programs to entice private parties to preserve wetlands, but these efforts face the same pressures. The Department of Agriculture funds a Water Bank Program, which pays landowners for protecting important waterfowl habitats (Baldwin, 1987, p. 19).

Slowly, and in piecemeal fashion, the federal government has whittled away the economic advantages of destroying wetlands. For example, before 1986, the federal tax code allowed farmers to deduct (as ordinary expense) the costs of draining or filling in wetlands. The 1986 Tax Reform Act contained a provision removing this deduction from the federal income tax, thereby making it more expensive for farmers to convert wetlands to alternative uses. Before 1985 federal agencies routinely provided flood and crop insurance to farmers who engaged in wetland drainage and fill. In 1985 the "swampbuster" program halted issuance of federal flood and crop insurance to farmers who converted wetland into farmland. However, even with these modest changes, the economic benefits of converting wetlands to alternative uses may still be much greater than the benefits from flood control, fish and wildlife refuge, or common recreation activities. Converting a wetland area into land that can be farmed, or on which a shopping mall can be built, promises substantial short-term economic benefit.

Another frequent problem with protecting the nation's wetlands occurs because different federal agencies have different orientations toward the environment. One of the agencies most responsible for the draining and filling of wetlands has been the U.S. Army Corps of Engineers, which has been involved in literally thousands of public works projects, many of which have affected wetland areas. Additionally, the Corps has responsibility for issuing permits for dredging or filling any waters in the United States. After the application for a permit, the Corps can issue the requested permit, deny it, or issue it with conditions. Typically, the Corps has done little to address the environmental impact of its actions. The National Environmental Policy Act of 1969, for the first time, required the Corps to conduct environmental impact assessments before embarking on any project. But it was not until the Clean Water Act of 1972 (section 404) was passed that legislation tried to coordinate the functions of the Corps and the EPA. The Corps has experienced significant change in philosophy and practice over the years (Mazmanian & Nienaber, 1979), but contrasts of philosophy with other wetlands protecting agencies remain.

Under current law, the issuance of these permits by the Corps is subject to EPA review. The EPA provides guidance to the Corps on policy and procedure in its review of the applications. The EPA has the authority to veto a permit after issuance, or even prohibit in advance permits for particular sites that are determined to be unsuited to dredge or fill activities (Platt, 1987, p. 17). This leads to one of the problems with implementation of wetlands protection, a problem of interagency coordination. As Baldwin (1987, p. 20) notes, "[i]n many places Corps districts and EPA regional offices work well together, but in others . . . cooperation is harder to see. The problem reflects basic policy conflicts." Administrators within the Corps often feel that shared responsibility does not provide an efficient means of protecting wetlands and have tried to limit EPA's actions. On the other hand, the EPA and other federal agencies seem to feel this joint effort offers a "most comprehensive opportunity to reduce wetland losses if given the chance" (Baldwin, 1987, p. 20).

Because two agencies are involved, it is difficult to devise either a speedy application review process or regulations and standards that are agreeable to all. This can be seen in problems associated with specific development proposals. For example, in July 1984 a developer in Attleboro, Massachusetts, requested a permit to fill in 32 acres of an inland wetlands under Section 404 of the Clean Water Act. As part of the application, the developer promised to construct and relocate an equal amount of artificially created wetlands. By May 1985 the Corps had decided to recommend that the permit be denied. In June, however, the permit was granted after the Corps' central office in Washington, D.C., had recommended reconsideration of the permit. In May 1986 EPA vetoed the Corps permit because the proposed creation of new wetlands by the developer was ill-specified; it was not clear whether it is possible to create artificial wetlands that perform the same functions as natural ones; and the policy of EPA was that functioning wetlands should not be filled in and used for non-water-oriented activities if "practicable" alternative sites for the proposed activities exist. Since the proposed development could conceivably be located in any of a number of areas, EPA revoked the permit.

While EPA policy was fairly clear, interagency coordination is still difficult to achieve. As Baldwin (1987, p. 20) points out, "EPA and the Corps still face disagreements over troublesome regulatory issues, such as what constitutes practicable alternatives to a wetland fill proposal, what non-water-dependent uses should receive permits, and what constitutes acceptable mitigation." It may seem strange that the Corps and EPA have not been able to fully reconcile their differences, but these differences appear deeply rooted in differing values. As noted in Chapter 1, environmental policy reflects a recurring clash of economics versus humanistic values. The differences between EPA and the Corps contain clear elements of this clash, where the EPA perhaps tended to advocate more humanistic values, while the Corps tended to advocate economic ones. This, as one might expect, often leads to delay and frustration on the part of many of the parties involved.

Many people have suggested that Section 404 of the Clean Water Act is in serious need of reform. It has been suggested that wetlands protection requires clearer definitions, allowance for state control of permit issuance, and strict guidelines for the roles of the Army Corps of Engineers and EPA. The Corps itself has pressed for changes, including shortening the time needed to review permit applications, increasing its ability to delegate authority to the states, and limiting its authority over certain wetlands (Ingram & Mann, 1984, p. 259). However, when the Clean Water Act was amended in 1987, no changes were made in this crucial section of the law, apparently because many interests wanted to avoid protracted debate (Baldwin, 1987, p. 39).

Water Policy and the States: Creative Answers to Some Difficult Problems?

Many people have criticized the Clean Water Act because of its attempt to impose uniform federal water quality and treatment standards on state and local governments. To many of these critics, federal water policy needs to provide a more flexible response, able to allow for differences in needs and conditions from state to state and region to region, especially differences in state and regional economies. Such critics often suggest that instead of simply providing federal funds for building municipal treatment facilities, legislation should make funds available to states, sub-state agencies, or interstate regional agencies to deal with the specific problems within that area. According to this argument, what is feasible or appropriate, in both economic and technical terms, for the Androscoggin River in Maine may not be for the Mississippi or Colorado rivers. What is right for the individual waterway and the region may be best determined at the state or sub-state level (or an interstate regional agency, in cases like the Mississippi where several states are involved). Perhaps there are certain waterways for which the standards should be higher; or one waterway that should receive more money than others due to its relative importance within the state or region.

Issues of the appropriate role of the federal government vis-à-vis state and local governments have also become a major problem in efforts to attack non-point sources water pollution. Non-point source water pollution consists of pollution that enters surface and groundwater from dispersed sources rather than concentrated sources. Non-point source pollution sources include: agricultural, where excess fertilizers, pesticides, insecticides, and fungicides may be carried by rain or irrigation water into lakes, streams, groundwater, and aquifers; storm water; and urban and building site runoff (Ingram & Mann, 1984, p. 257). As described previously, most federal water control efforts have focused on point source pollution—where federal efforts concentrate on influencing states to regulate the effluent discharges from specific polluting parties. Yet it has been estimated that perhaps half of the water pollution in America's water is from non-point sources (Freeman, 1978, p. 52). Indeed, as point sources of water pollution are effectively regulated, non-point sources account for an ever larger share of unchecked pollution. So why has so little federal effort been focused on non-point source water pollution?

The reason why the federal government is not deeply involved in non-point source water pollution regulation is that most of the states and many members of Congress do not want such involvement. Although control of non-point pollution sources is a major technical challenge, they do not want such involvement for reasons related to land use and zoning decisions (Ingram & Mann, pp. 257-258). Traditionally, in America decisions about land use and zoning fall to the responsibility of local and state governments. It is extremely rare for the federal government to directly prohibit the use of a particular piece of land for a particular purpose. Yet, for the EPA to become involved in non-point source pollution control would require it to dictate whether a piece of land could be used for agriculture or another purpose that results in water pollution, an involvement that is politically unacceptable to many people.

So the EPA continues to search for ways to affect non-point source water pollution without directly intervening in land use decisions. Much of this search focuses on trying to entice the states to take initiative against such pollution sources. The EPA's efforts have been limited to working with states, gathering information, monitoring water pollution, and providing technical assistance to state agencies. EPA action tends to focus on trying to protect aquifers that provide the only source of water for large population areas, monitoring and testing groundwater around hazardous waste sites, and trying to ensure that commercial development projects assess their impact on water supplies (Jessup, pp. 11-12). Setting priorities for non-point source pollution control is essentially left to the states (Ingram & Mann, p. 258).

Still, the states have sometimes taken much more initiative toward protecting and improving water quality than required by EPA. Whenever states exercise authority delegated by the EPA, the states are free to impose more stringent requirements than called for in federal standards, which they sometimes do. A number of states have taken initiative to regulate water contaminants beyond those taken by the EPA. For example, some states have used the EPA's recommended maximum contaminant level guidelines or have developed their own standards to write their own regulations (National Research Council, 1986b). So at least several states, including New York, New Jersey, Wisconsin, Florida, and Massachusetts, have opted to set water contamination standards when the EPA has not.

In recent times, many federal/state efforts at coordinated water management have emerged. For example, the federal Congressional Office of Technology Assessment has identified a number of developing water management programs involving efforts of individual states, groups of states, and the EPA working with states. These include the Chesapeake Bay Program, which involves the EPA and the states of Maryland, Virginia, Pennsylvania, and other federal agencies; the Puget Sound Water Quality Authority, a Washington State-funded program; and others. However, despite the seemingly innovative efforts by states, sometimes working with EPA and with sub-state or regional authorities, there is not a great deal of evidence that they have been able to actually improve the quality of water (Wagner, 1988).

The Processes of Making Federal Water Policy

The brief description of the evolution and current status of water pollution legislation in the United States provides a basic background to American water policy. With this basic background to the various pieces of federal legislation that help define federal water policy, the policy-making processes associated with this legislation constitute important elements of water policy. Up until now, very little has been written about how and why the various legislation was enacted. Although space does not permit an in-depth discussion of each piece of legislation, the policy-making processes associated with two major pieces of federal legislation might serve as useful examples. The Federal Water Pollution Control Act Amendments of 1972 and the Municipal Wastewater Treatment Construction Grant Amendments Act of 1981 provide two such examples. For each, there will first be a description of the policy formulation and adoption processes, that is, the politics associated with congressional decisions to put the underlying problem on the public agenda and to enact this legislation. This will be followed by an examination of problems of implementation, focusing on how and why some of the more controversial aspects of federal water policy evolved. In particular, the study will review why the federal role in water policy changed from one of pursuing nothing more than state cooperation, to one of imposing federal standards and regulations on state and local governments, and back to one of deference to the states.

The Federal Water Pollution Control Act Amendments of 1972

As noted earlier, the Federal Water Pollution Control Act Amendments of 1972 marked something of a watershed in national water policy because they represented a major change in the way the federal government affected water quality and pollution issues in this country. Examining the adoption of this piece of legislation can contribute to an understanding of how and why the federal government began to embark on this expansion of federal authority and responsibility. The policy-making process model, a general version of which was described in Chapter 2, can serve as the organizing framework for this examination. Thus, the conditions that seemed to lend themselves to consideration of a fairly radical change in water policy, the problem formation stage, are delineated. Then an effort is made to examine the policy formulation, adoption, and implementation processes.

The Problem Formation Process

The 1972 Clean Water Act was produced as a result of a specific confluence of events. Concern about water pollution certainly paralleled that of other types of pollution, especially air pollution, which had been dealt with in 1970. The context for the enactment of a new and stricter federal law included fairly widespread recognition that earlier efforts, especially through the Federal Water Pollution Control Act of 1956 and its amendments, simply did not work. There was mounting evidence that earlier efforts to reduce industrial water pollution, which called for negotiation with polluters to voluntarily make significant reductions in their effluent discharges, did not work (Caldwell & Roos, 1971; Roos & Bohner, 1973). Earlier legislation and its implementation resulted not in cleaner water, but in repeated disputes between the federal and state agencies. Efforts to develop water quality standards serve as a prime example of what caused the federal/state disputes.

This earlier legislation called for states to establish their own clean water standards and submit them to the Federal Water Quality Control Administration (FWCA) for approval. Once approved, these standards were to become federal standards with federal enforcement. State water quality standards were supposed to be submitted and approved by the end of June 1967; however, it took the FWCA more than a year and a half just to develop guidelines for the states to follow in submitting their standards for federal review. This left the states with very little time (6 months at most) to actually prepare their standards (Lieber, 1975, p. 21). Obviously, the states articulated considerable dissatisfaction with this process. As this legislation neared its scheduled expiration, it became increasingly likely that Congress would not simply extend it.

In addition to the dissatisfaction with the effectiveness of existing water policy, environmental interest groups, which began to come into their own in terms of political influence, made it clear that they felt a stronger federal role would be necessary if the quality of the water was to be improved. Added to this was the recognition by members of Congress that the existence of a number of disparate pieces of federal legislation, including the River and Harbor Act of 1899 (which was commonly called the Refuse Act of 1899), made it desirable to find a way to integrate federal regulatory standards—to in effect develop a single set of water quality standards, rather than having a number of separate federal programs, each with its own set of standards. These conditions made Congress receptive to proposals for rather radical

changes in federal water policy. As Lieber (p. 29) states, these conditions created "a period that closely corresponded with Downs' second
stage in the issue attention cycle—Alarmed Discovery and Euphoric
Enthusiasm," described in Chapter 2.

The Policy Formulation and Adoption Processes

With the conditions virtually set for consideration in new water
legislation, the policy formulation stage becomes the focus of attention.
In the case of the formulation process leading up to the 1972 Clean
Water Act, proposals emerged from a number of different sources.
Perhaps the most important sources were the U.S. Senate, especially
Senator Edmund Muskie (D-Maine), the chairman of the Air and Water
Pollution subcommittee of the Senate Public Works Committee, and the
Nixon administration. In 1970 and 1971 both Muskie and the Nixon
administration had proposed a number of different pieces of legislation
calling for stricter water quality standards from the states, including
standards to be applied to individual polluters, stricter enforcement
provisions and penalties, expanded water treatment facility construction grants, and even the creation of an Environmental Financing
Authority to purchase local waste treatment facility bonds.

Before new legislation was enacted, however, Congress had passed
the 1970 Clean Air Act Amendments (discussed in Chapter 3). These
amendments provided a clear precedent for the design of new water
pollution legislation. The same Senate subcommittee, on Air and Water
Pollution, held jurisdiction over legislation in both areas. After having
recently completed work on the Clean Air Act, this subcommittee and
its chair, Edmund Muskie, borrowed many provisions from the Clean
Air Act in defining the federal role. So initial proposals introduced into
the Senate called for uniform national standards rather than different
standards for each state; states to ensure compliance and enforce the
federal standards through state implementation plans; and state implementation plans to be reviewed and approved by EPA.

At about the same time, efforts were being made to pass legislation
in the House of Representatives. However, the House, through its Public
Works Committee and its chair, John Blatnik (D-Minnesota), wanted to
pursue a much less radical change to existing legislation. While the
House adopted new legislation, the resulting version retained considerably greater flexibility toward the states, especially in the permit process. Instead of allowing EPA the authority to review each permit issued

under state permit programs, the House version precluded EPA action unless the entire state permitting program were revoked. Thus, the House bill leaned away from uniform standards and emphasized state activity over federal activity.

After passage of the disparate House and Senate versions of new water pollution control legislation, conferees from each body met 39 times to resolve the differences. Compromise was not easily reached, especially with respect to the permit program. A final version was hammered out, allowing the EPA to revoke a state's permit under two conditions: if a state-issued permit allowed pollution discharge outside of the guidelines of requirements of the EPA; or if a governor of one state reported his/her state adversely affected by pollution from another state. On October 4, 1972, the House of Representatives passed the conference compromise by a margin of 366 to 11, and the Senate passed it by 74 to 0. Then the Federal Water Pollution Act Amendments of 1972 were sent to President Nixon for his signature.

Nixon's initial inclination was to veto this legislation because the grants program in the Act was roughly three times the amount originally built into the administration's proposals. The final bill authorized some $18 billion for grants to state and local governments for facility construction from 1973 through 1975, while the Nixon administration requested about $6 billion. EPA Chief administrator William Ruckelshaus favored signing the Act and communicated that position to the White House. Nevertheless, Nixon, saying that he felt compelled to oppose any bill calling for drastically higher spending, vetoed the Act less than an hour before it would have automatically become law. Apparently, Nixon realized, in an election year, he could oppose greater spending, thereby shifting the blame to Congress, where the margins of passage in the House and Senate were more than enough to override his veto.

On October 18, the House voted 247 to 23 and the Senate voted 52 to 12 to override the President's veto. With this action, the Federal Water Pollution Control Act Amendments of 1972 became law. Rosenbaum (1985, p. 168) suggests that the popularity of this Act came largely from including the $18-million grant program designed to help local municipal waste facility construction. As he states, the grant program "was the carrot that accompanied the regulatory stick to make federal regulatory programs palatable to state and local governments." This grant program provided something that nearly all members of Congress supported because it provided potential benefits to cities and towns in virtually every member's district. Thus, the popularity of this approach in Congress is tied directly to its pork barrel features.

At the same time, this approach started a federal commitment that was difficult to change. The grant program provided funds that benefited many people, including those who were involved in the construction and operation of municipal or regional sewage treatment facilities. According to Rosenbaum (p. 168), this legislation nurtured a vigorous coalition of interest groups, each having a stake in the program, including the Association of Metropolitan Sewage Agencies, the National Utility Contractors Association, and the Association of State and Interstate Water Pollution Control Administrators. Thus, it helped create and maintain political support for its own continuation.

Difficulties in Implementing National Water Policy

A recurring issue in federal water policy, as described here, involves the tension between being flexible on the one hand, and holding state and local governments accountable for actually protecting and improving water quality on the other hand. The dilemma is that for states wishing to avoid making water quality improvements, such flexibility often provides the mechanism to do so. Yet the inflexibility associated with uniform federal standards has often produced two related results: It seldom adequately allows states the leeway they need to take what, for them, would be perhaps the most effective actions to improve or protect the water; and governors and other state officials argue that it may force states to take actions that impede the efficient operation of their private economies. There is no part of the policy-making process where this tension has had a greater presence than in implementation.

As noted earlier, the Clean Water Act of 1972 and its Amendments serve as the statutory foundation for the EPA's authority in regulating water pollution. The EPA has used this authority to develop regulations, or guidelines, specifying the standards for and limits on permissible pollution discharges from industrial sources. These guidelines also specify the kinds of technologies that must be used to meet these pollution discharge limits. The 1987 Amendments require industries to comply with any effluent emissions limitations within 3 years after EPA issues these regulations. However, the exact regulations, standards, and limitations that EPA has established under these laws have not been examined in great detail. Yet these limitations and standards form the core and substance of federal environmental water pollution policy. So, a little closer look at these regulations, and where possible, the administrative process EPA went through to establish these regulations, will augment this description of national water policy.

Fleeting references have been made to the standards and limits developed under various water legislation, especially the 1972 Clean Water Act, but such references have not been very specific about what these regulations look like. Most of the regulations emerging from the Clean Water Act and its amendments are referred to as guidelines, where efforts are directed toward specifying the *technologies* various polluting parties must use to clean up water before it can be discharged. Current EPA regulations set technology-based standards for three different kinds of pollutants: conventional pollutants, including substances that are known to deplete oxygen content of the waters into which the pollutant is being discharged, substances that affect the level of acidity of the water, and substances such as suspended solid materials, fecal matter, oil, and grease; toxic pollutants, mostly hazardous chemicals and chemical wastes, that are among the EPA's approximately 130 priority toxic pollutants; and nonconventional pollutants, including ammonia, chlorine, iron, phosphorous, and a class of chemicals known as phenols. Pollutants in each of these categories are treated differently.

The EPA requires parties involved with discharging these three types of substances to use specific technologies to make these substances "cleaner" (less toxic, hazardous, or damaging) before they can be discharged. There are currently five categories of technology that parties can be required to use:

1. Best Practicable Technology: This has been set as the minimum acceptable level of effluent treatment for existing industrial and waste treatment facilities before materials can be discharged into surface water. Most facilities currently meet this standard.

2. Best Conventional Technology: This is more stringent than the "best practicable technology" requirement. The 1977 Amendments to the Clean Water Act specified that parties discharging "conventional pollutants" should meet this standard by July 1, 1984, but the EPA has not yet issued regulations covering all conventional pollutants.

3. Best Available Technology: This is the most stringent requirement and applies to "priority toxic" and "nonconventional" pollutants. Parties discharging these types of pollutants were also supposed to meet this require-

ment by July 1, 1984, but to date, EPA has issued only a few of the necessary specific regulations for these chemicals.

4. Best Professional Judgment: This is a rather vague requirement that applies to discharges of types of substances for which EPA has not issued specific regulations.
5. Best Available Demonstrated Control Technology: This is a requirement that generally applies to parties (industries) constructing new manufacturing or other facilities. It basically requires parties constructing such facilities to install state-of-the-art technology, whatever it happens to be at the time construction is undertaken.

Decisions about what specific kinds of technologies should be applied to which chemicals are made at least in part based on some form of risk assessment. As noted by National Research Council (1983, p. 43), "risk assessment may be used to show the human exposure that corresponds to a specific degree of risk or to calculate the risk remaining after control technologies are put in place." In other words, the required technology is, according to risk analysis, presumably one that would yield discharges into waterways that pose little or no danger to people who might be exposed to that water.

Regulations emerging from the Safe Drinking Water Act and its amendments are somewhat different than those emerging from the Clean Water Act amendments. The Safe Drinking Water Act requires the EPA to identify and regulate any contaminants in water supplies that may have adverse effect on the health of persons. EPA is also supposed to examine such contaminants and determine at what level these substances would produce "no known or anticipated adverse effects" on people. These relatively safe levels of contamination are supposed to be achieved "to the extent feasible" after taking into consideration a variety of engineering and economic factors (Regens, Dietz, & Rycroft, 1983, p. 140).

When Congress enacted the Safe Drinking Water Act, it was anticipated that safe levels of contamination could and would be established scientifically. The National Academy of Sciences (NAS) was involved in studying a whole range of contaminants, and Congress apparently expected the result of this study to include Recommended Maximum Contaminant Levels for specific chemicals, which presumably EPA could simply build into its regulations. However, after studying many of these chemicals, the NAS concluded that such safe levels of contaminants could not be determined scientifically. As a result, EPA has had to use a variety of risk assessment and health effects information to try to derive specific regulations (Regens, Dietz, & Rycroft, p. 140). To date, the EPA has issued regulations for only a small number of chemicals. The 1988 legislation specified that the EPA should set standards for at least 25 contaminants by January 1991, a deadline that it missed.

The Safe Drinking Water Act did, however, require the EPA to publish a list of chemicals that would be candidates for possible future regulation. In preparing this list, the EPA actually opted at the same time to comply with a provision of the Superfund Amendments and Reauthorization Act of 1986 (SARA), which required the development of a list of hazardous substances found in hazardous waste sites. The 1991 list of priority contaminants under the Safe Drinking Water Act (presented in Table 4.2), for example, was based in part on the list prepared under SARA.

Compliance With and Enforcement of Water Quality Standards

Perhaps the greatest problem with water policy implementation exists as it relates to municipal waste treatment facilities. Federal water pollution policy was based in part on the assumption that if the federal government provided the funds to build modern waste treatment facilities, and these facilities were actually constructed, the facilities would almost automatically meet effluent discharge limits specified in their permits. Consequently, the quality of the water would improve. However, analysis by the U.S. General Accounting Office (GAO, 1980) suggests that there are flaws in this expectation. In 1979 the GAO randomly selected and analyzed some 242 waste treatment plants in the Boston, Chicago, and San Francisco metropolitan areas (GAO, 1980). These plants were monitored for one year, and the results of the analysis showed that 87% (211) violated the terms of their effluent discharge permits for at least one month out of the year. Moreover, 56% of the facilities violated their permits for more than 6 months out of the year. Detailed analyses of the 211 facilities in violation for at least one month revealed that almost one-third committed what the GAO referred to as "serious" violations.

While there are many cases of enforcement problems, there is little systematic evidence concerning broader patterns of the EPA's enforcement activities. To investigate such patterns, and to see whether the EPA exhibited any sort of bias in the way it enforced the Clean Water Act, Yeager (1987) studied enforcement activities of the EPA against more

Table 4.2 The 1991 Priority List of Contaminants Under the Safe Drinking Water Act Amendments of 1988

Inorganic Substances
  Aluminum
  Boron
  Chloramines
  Chlorate
  Chlorine
  Chlorine dioxide
  Chlorite
  Cyanogen chloride
  Hypochlorite ion
  Manganese
  Molybdenum
  Strontium
  Vanadium
  Zinc
Pesticides
  Asulam
  Bentazon
  Bromacil
  Cyanazine
  DCPA (and its acid metabolites)
  Dicamba
  Ethylenethiourea
  Fomesafen
  Lactofen/Acifluorfen
  Metalaxyl
  Methomyl
  Metolachlor
  Metribuzin
  Parathion degradation product
  Prometon
  2,4,5-T
  Thiodicarb
  Trifluralin
Synthetic Organic Chemicals
  Acrylonitrile
  Bromobenzene
  Bromochloroacetonitrite
  Bromodichloromethane
  Bromoform

Bromomethane
Chlorination/Chloramination
  by-products
Chloroethane
Chloroform
Chloropicrin
o-Chlorotoluene
p-Chlorotoluene
Dibromoacetonitrile
Dibromochloromethane
Dibromomethane
Dichloroacetonitrile
1,3-Dichlorobenzene
Dichlorodifluoromethane
1,1-Dichlorethane
2,2-Dichloropropane
1,3-Dichloropropane
1,1-Dichloropropene
1,3-Dichloropropene
2,4-Dinitrophenol
2,4-Dinitrotoluene
2,6-Dinitrotoluene
1,2-Diphenylhydrazine
Fluorotrichloromethane
Hexachlorobutadiene
Hexachloroethane
Isophorone
Methyl ethyl ketone
Methyl isobutyl ketone
Methyl-t-butyl ether
Naphthalene
Nitrobenzene
Ozone by-products
1,1,1,2-Tetrachloroethane
1,1,2,2-Tetrachloroethane
Tetrahydrofuran
Trichloroacetonitrile
1,2,3-Trichloropropane
Microorganisms
  Cryptosporidum

than 100 American-owned manufacturing firms in New Jersey. He analyzed the number of serious effluent violations each firm had committed,
and the nature of sanctions EPA might have brought against the firm,
between 1973 and 1978. He found that water quality regulations tended to
disproportionately affect small and medium-size companies, with larger
companies much better able to comply. He also found that enforcement
actions were taken disproportionately against smaller firms, since larger
companies are able to mobilize resources to fight enforcement, especially
through expensive litigation. Not surprisingly, this research suggests that
technology-based water quality regulation puts smaller and midsize polluters at something of a financial disadvantage, compared to larger firms.

The Adoption of the Municipal Wastewater Treatment Construction Grant (Clean Water Act) Amendments of 1981

Despite the political support that may have been nurtured by the 1972
Clean Water Act's grants program, as described earlier, this program was
changed considerably in 1981, with the passage of the Municipal Wastewater Treatment Construction Grant Amendments. It was suggested previously that this Act marked the start of a somewhat reduced federal role
in financing water quality improvements. Partly because evaluations of
whether the earlier grants program contributed to cleaner water, and partly
because of the new zeal that the Reagan administration brought to Washington to cut federal spending, this Act trimmed the grants program
considerably. Even by the late 1970s, a major federal evaluation of more
than 200 completed sewage treatment facilities in 10 states revealed that
about 80% were still violating at least one federal effluent standard.
Consequently, the Reagan administration sought to drastically reduce the
federal role in local and regional facility construction.

The initial Reagan administration proposal called for eliminating the
grants program, and even sought to cut off federal funding for projects
already under construction. When legislation was introduced, the House
of Representatives' version "grandfathered in" such facilities, but President Reagan threatened to veto any legislation that contained such a
provision, mainly because it would have more than doubled the cost. So
Congress eventually settled on a much reduced program, rather than face
elimination of the entire grants program (CQWR, 1981, pp. 2527-2529).

While there seemed to have been clear sentiment in the Senate to
support the reduced budget in the administration's proposal, at least one
Senator, John Chaffee (R-Rhode Island) apparently wanted to have it

both ways. The Senate version provided a $200-million fund to correct runoff from combined storm and sewage systems—a fund designed to primarily benefit the city of Providence, Rhode Island, in Chaffee's home state. At the same time, Buddy Roemer (D-Louisiana) strongly favored the House version's provision allotting federal money to help fix leaky pipes. As the result of a conference compromise, the final legislation contained both of these provisions (CQWR, 1981, p. 2527).

Water Policy in America: A Summary

America's water policy has been described here as consisting of a variety of pieces of legislation and actions by federal, state, and local agencies. Such legislation and agency activity focus on many different aspects of water quality and protection, including efforts to limit disposal of hazardous materials into local sewage treatment facilities and waterways, to specify required levels of treatment that effluent discharges must receive before being discharged, to protect groundwater and surface water, and to preserve delicate and important wetlands.

To understand the nature of public policy toward water, it is necessary to examine not only the legislation on which such policy is based, but also the actions by implementing agencies. Throughout federal environmental policy, there has been a clear tension between trying to establish national standards to be applied to polluting parties, trying to be flexible enough to permit the federal laws to help improve and protect the quality of water rather than getting in the way of this goal, and trying to make sure that flexibility is not used by states and/or individual polluters as a mechanism for failing to work toward improving and protecting the water.

The tensions that have become characteristic of federal water policy illustrate several of the clashes of values described in Chapter 1. When Congress decided to enact strong new legislation in 1972, giving the EPA authority to impose its regulations on states and individual polluting parties, the tension between economic efficiency and humanism was clearly present. When the EPA tried to be very aggressive in applying the law to the states, tensions concerning the role of government in society were clearly evident. When the EPA, under the Reagan administration, backed away from vigorous enforcement of water regulations, it did so partly because it reflected one side in the clash of values involving the role of government, especially the federal government, in society.

Many of these same tensions will continue to be associated with federal and state water pollution policies in the future. At best, governmental agencies and legislatures are able to strike an uneasy balance among interests that frequently disagree over protection of water resources. Efforts to improve water quality progress at a snail's pace. At worst, stalemate between competing interests and values produces policies that probably benefit no interest and also fail to protect America's water supplies. In between, one interest or another captures the policy-making process for a short time, often reversing previous policies, only to lose control at a later time. The consequence is that public water policy experiences fits and starts, and only sporadically progresses toward protecting and improving water quality.

As water pollution and supply problems become more acute, there will be continuing controversies over who should have access to existing water and who will pay the cost of improving water quality or supply—just as there has been considerable debate over which level of government should be responsible for water protection policies, and which level of government should pay for such policies. States will likely continue to advocate that the federal government should pay for water quality improvements, but the federal government should not impose strings on how they use the money. Thus, states frequently want to receive the benefits of the policy without having to pay for them directly. The "who pays" question becomes even more difficult when water supply issues are involved. In the West, the operant philosophy and water rights laws lead to apparent overuse of water supplies, providing a never-ending source of pressure on the federal government to help finance new water diversion projects; yet federal involvement in specifying appropriate water uses or allocations remains totally unacceptable. These controversies will not disappear any time soon.

There have been some water quality issues not addressed in this chapter. The impact of acid rain on groundwater, and policies to affect this impact, were discussed in earlier chapters. Another area not addressed in this chapter is public policies to protect groundwater from toxic wastes. Obviously, groundwater quality is threatened by the existence of toxic wastes disposed of in the ground. Public policies toward toxic waste disposal are, at least in part, motivated by a desire to protect groundwater sources. However, issues surrounding toxic and hazardous waste deserve a fuller treatment than would be afforded by inclusion here, so they will be addressed in Chapter 5.

5

Public Policies Toward Contaminating the Soil
Regulating Hazardous Wastes and Toxic Substances

O ver the past decade and a half, there have been few environmental issues of greater importance than those associated with hazardous and toxic wastes. As discussed in Chapter 1, problems of hazardous and toxic waste possess many dimensions and are considered problems for many different reasons. Hazardous wastes may be handled in a way that creates immediate health threats by virtue of inadvertently allowing people to be exposed to them. Not uncommonly, the improper handling of hazardous wastes affects people's health by contaminating sources of drinking water. There have been many instances where people's lives have been unalterably changed by the improper handling of hazardous wastes and materials.

As noted in Chapter 2, considerable public concern developed during the 1960s over hazardous chemicals in the environment through the much-publicized accounts of the effects of the pesticide DDT. Until the strange happenings in Love Canal, New York, there had not been much public awareness of the harmful effects of toxic waste disposal (Levine,

1982). In this widely publicized case, toxic wastes that had escaped from a dump in an abandoned canal had seeped into hundreds of private homes and an elementary school, and the entire neighborhood had suffered from unexplainable illnesses. It took years for the residents to become mobilized and obtain any sort of positive response and recognition from public officials. Eventually, several hundred residents of the area were forced to evacuate their homes. Other similar experiences were repeated in hundreds of places around the country (Cohen, 1984, p. 276).

As the general public learned of the events surrounding Love Canal, naïveté and ignorance were replaced by distrust of how American industries were handling hazardous substances, and skepticism about how effectively the public sector was able to regulate them. This distrust of industry, along with a recognition that government should do more to find out how serious the hazardous waste problem really was, fueled a number of efforts to stimulate federal action. These and many other events, such as the discovery in 1982 of massive dioxin contamination in Times Beach, Missouri, helped to move hazardous waste problems squarely onto the public agenda. To a degree never experienced before, public officials and industry began to search for some solution to this problem. Of course not everyone perceived that there was in fact a problem. But by and large, by the early 1980s there had developed a fairly clear consensus that steps would have to be taken to alleviate the health threat from toxic chemicals.

This is not to say that everyone agreed on which chemicals are hazardous or at what levels. Not everyone agreed about how fast action should be taken. Moreover, as an extension of the Reagan administration's simultaneous pursuit of overall deregulation and shift of responsibilities from the federal to state governments, people disagreed about the role of the federal EPA in toxics policy (Cohen, 1984). Nevertheless, there developed some degree of consensus that something had to be done, that toxic and hazardous wastes posed a significant enough health risk that government action was desirable.

This consensus has led the federal government to pursue a four-pronged approach. The first prong stems from the immediate concern about cleaning up existing toxic threats. For example, it became increasingly clear that the traditional ways of handling hazardous wastes, to dump them into waterways or bury them under the ground, were creating major health risk problems rather than solving them. Thus, Superfund was born with the notion that hazardous waste sites—places where significant amounts of hazardous materials had been dumped, buried, or abandoned—would be identified, analyzed, and cleaned up. However, it was also recognized that this approach did nothing about future threats. Clearly the existing threats were seen as the product of the poor practices of the past, and unless these practices were changed in the present, new problems would continue to be created into the future.

Thus, the second prong focused on what is usually called "waste minimization" or "source reduction" strategies. This simply reflects the idea that too much hazardous chemical waste is being produced, and that the magnitude of the problem can be reduced, perhaps to a more manageable level, by diminishing not only the amounts of chemical and hazardous materials indiscriminately used in the environment but also wastes requiring disposal. As applied to hazardous wastes, much of this focuses on incentives for getting industry to alter its manufacturing processes so that less toxic waste is produced as by-products. In terms of hazardous materials, especially pesticides, insecticides, and fungicides, it focuses on constraining and limiting their uses. Simultaneously it calls for sanctions, as manifested in clearly fixed liability found in many pieces of legislation, for producers of hazardous chemical wastes to dispose of wastes properly. It also focused on getting people to understand that a large portion of the problem of improper chemical and hazardous waste disposal comes from the home. Many people seemed to believe that source reduction might by itself constitute a complete solution to the problems of the future. Yet at some point numerous studies made it fairly clear that simply altering the various manufacturing and technical processes, along with practices within the home, would not likely reduce the stream of hazardous wastes to a manageable level, given existing technologies (O'Hare, 1984).

The third prong of the federal solution called for increasing corporate accountability in the handling of hazardous chemical wastes. This approach was stimulated by the belief that producers of hazardous chemical wastes were essentially acting irresponsibly by burying their problems underground or dumping them into our waterways. Thus, the obvious answer was to regulate the handling of such wastes by requiring producers to document and keep precise records of what they did with them. Federal laws were written to make this a requirement. Additionally, major efforts were made to license landfills so that the only ones to accept such wastes would be those that could reasonably be considered "secure," or unlikely to allow toxic chemicals buried there to leach into the groundwater or otherwise become health dangers. Increasingly, enforcement of landfill disposal regulations closed off disposal options for producers. This, naturally, stimulated attempts to find alternative disposal opportunities.

This leads to the fourth prong of the solution: developing hazardous waste treatment facilities. Under this piece of the solution, chemical wastes would be subjected to chemical processes that would render them nontoxic, or at least less toxic than before. In most cases, the products of such processes could be safely disposed of in the final instance through such existing techniques as landfills. The chemical processes to which toxic substances would be subjected, of course, would vary widely, depending on the toxic in question. In some cases, reusable industrial products would be extracted and resold, as with solvent recovery plants. In other cases, toxics would be incinerated at very high temperatures to render them less toxic. Different processes would be applied to different toxic chemicals.

These four prongs of the federal policy toward hazardous and toxic wastes are found in a variety of legislation and related programs. Before examining these four strategies directly, it might be helpful to review the legislation that largely forms the basis for these strategies. In this way, it will be possible to see the evolution of federal hazardous waste policy and its underlying strategies.

Federal Hazardous Waste-Related Legislation

There are many pieces of federal legislation related to hazardous waste, some of which have already been addressed in previous chapters. In Chapter 3, for example, the EPA acted out of the 1970 Clean Air Act Amendments to define a number of hazardous and toxic substances found in air pollution. Chapter 4 described EPA efforts, stemming from the 1986 Safe Drinking Water Act, to protect water supplies from hazardous wastes. However, there have been a number of very important pieces of legislation directed explicitly to the problems of hazardous waste production, handling, and disposal. Table 5.1 provides a list of the key federal legislation relating to hazardous wastes enacted since 1965.

Prior to the mid-1970s, the disposal of hazardous wastes was treated much like that of other types of solid wastes, and hazardous waste was not considered a distinct type of waste. Hazardous waste disposal was

Table 5.1 Major Federal Hazardous and Toxic Waste Legislation Since 1965

The Solid Waste Disposal Act of 1965

The Resource Recovery Act of 1970

The Federal Environmental Pesticide Control Act of 1972

The Resource Conservation and Recovery Act of 1976 (RCRA)
  (Also referred to as the Solid Waste Disposal Amendments of 1976)

The Toxic Substances Control Act of 1976 (TSCA)

The Federal Environmental Pesticide Control Act Amendments of 1978

The Comprehensive Environmental Response, Compensation, and Liability Act of
  1980 (CERCLA)

The Hazardous and Solid Waste Amendments Act of 1984

The Superfund Amendments and Reauthorization Act of 1986 (SARA)

---

covered by the 1965 Solid Waste Disposal Act and the 1970 Resource Recovery Act (RRA). The 1965 Act established a national research program to investigate effective means of disposing of solid waste, especially household and industrial paper waste. The RRA promoted, through research and demonstration projects, the recycling of solid wastes. Neither of these Acts defined hazardous wastes, and with reference to the RRA, Rosenbaum (1977, p. 271) suggests that it was "a feeble yet mildly constructive Congressional initiative toward waste management." This Act largely focused on recycling solid waste, and like federal legislation in other pollution areas, provided some modest technical assistance to state and local governments in developing their own waste recovery programs.

The federal role in hazardous and toxic waste policy started in earnest with several major pieces of federal legislation beginning in the mid-1970s. The first of these, the Resource Conservation and Recovery Act of 1976 (RCRA), also known at the time of enactment as the Solid Waste Disposal Amendments of 1976, revised and amended the 1965 Solid Waste Disposal Act and the 1970 Resource Recovery Act. Perhaps the most significant of its provisions focused on the management and disposal of hazardous wastes. It was designed to ensure that hazardous substances were not disposed of without regard for potential public health consequences. This Act made the first real attempt to distinguish and define what kinds of materials constitute hazardous wastes. It broadly defined a hazardous waste as:

[A]ny solid waste, or combination of solid wastes, that, because of its quantity, concentration, or physical, chemical, or infectious characteristics (1) cause, or significantly contribute to, an increase in mortality or an increase in serious, irreversible, or incapacitating reversible, illness; or (2) pose a substantial present of potential hazard to human health or the environment when improperly treated, stored, transported, or disposed of, or otherwise managed.

As will be discussed in the context of the implementation of this Act, the EPA issued regulations that gave this definition considerable detail.

This Act provided for the regulation of hazardous wastes through six major components. First, it called on the EPA to identify and make public a list of substances considered to be hazardous when disposed. Second, it created the "cradle to grave" system of tracking hazardous materials. Third, it regulated the transportation of hazardous chemicals. Fourth, it authorized the EPA to set standards for the storage, treatment, and disposal of hazardous wastes. Fifth, it created a permit system for any handlers of hazardous wastes. And sixth, it authorized the EPA to establish guidelines to govern state hazardous waste management programs. The Act also had provisions calling for EPA to regulate underground storage tanks containing hazardous wastes.

One of the keystones of the actual regulation of hazardous wastes was the "cradle to grave" tracking system. This system sought to protect the public from exposure to improperly disposed of hazardous materials by requiring the tracking of hazardous substances from the time they are created until the time they are disposed of—from their "cradle to grave." Taken together, the Act's provisions would allow the EPA or state agencies to track any material defined as hazardous from the time it was manufactured or produced to the time it was finally disposed of. This requires the keeping of detailed records by any party involved in operating facilities that treat, store, transport, or dispose of hazardous materials, and also requires monitoring and inspecting these facilities. The Act also called for the EPA to specify standards for the location, design, construction, and operation of all facilities involved in the treatment, storage, or disposal of hazardous wastes.

Also in 1976 Congress passed the Toxic Substances Control Act (TSCA) in an attempt to help create a Western European-style policy, which would limit what private sector chemical manufacturers did with their products or by-products. This Act was designed to hold chemical manufacturers responsible for providing the EPA with information so that any chemical's potential health hazards could be tested before it was marketed. The Act authorized the EPA to prevent the marketing of any chemical that was found to pose an "imminent hazard" to people's health. In order to make this determination, the Act authorized the establishment of an Interagency Testing Committee to identify and recommend to the EPA chemical substances that should be tested for possible imminent hazards. This legislation has not been very effective, largely because there are no clear-cut testing procedures or standards to determine whether a chemical does indeed present an imminent hazard, and because many companies have claimed that their products are proprietary—that they and only they have a right to know what the chemicals are (Davis & Lester, 1988, p. 27).

Perhaps the best known major piece of legislation, the Comprehensive Environmental Response, Compensation, and Liability Act of 1980 (CERCLA), established what has become known as "Superfund," a pool of $1.6 billion to help finance cleanup of existing hazardous waste sites and chemical spills. It was to be financed through a special tax on waste producers. It also established liability in the law for recovery of cleanup costs from responsible parties, including multiple parties in instances where precise responsibility for the waste is difficult to prove. It also required the EPA to establish a priority listing, called the National Priorities List, of hazardous waste sites that needed to be cleaned up. The first National Priorities List was issued in 1982. Periodically, EPA revises the priority list to add newly discovered sites or to remove cleaned-up (remediated) sites. This Act also sought to create a comprehensive management information system to record and maintain data about chemical and hazardous waste dump sites. The resulting information system, called the Emergency and Remedial Response Information System (ERRIS), was to be used to help EPA inventory and prioritize sites for possible cleanup. These two Acts, RCRA and CERCLA, were our first real national public policy responses to the elevated place hazardous waste issues assumed on the public agenda.

RCRA was amended and altered in 1984 with the passage of the Hazardous and Solid Waste Amendments, which clarified and extended the EPA's jurisdiction over the regulation of hazardous wastes. According to Fortuna and Lennett (1987, p. 7), these Amendments constitute "what many consider the most significant rewrite of any environmental law." This Act "legislated fundamental changes in the regulatory program, in an overwhelmingly bipartisan manner, without Reagan administration support, at a time when other environmental laws were languishing in

Congress," to overcome the fact that the EPA had no coherent vision of what an effective hazardous waste management strategy should look like.

Apparently, these Amendments were enacted by Congress out of general dissatisfaction with EPA's progress and enthusiasm in implementing RCRA. The specific problems of implementation will be discussed in more detail later. However, it became clear to many that the EPA was willing to set standards under RCRA only to the extent that it had to by meeting the letter of the law. It did issue a few standards sufficient to meet what the law specifically required, but many of the regulations were narrowly targeted; contained many loopholes, including exemptions from many kinds of hazardous waste and small generators of wastes; and did not address some of the more serious hazardous waste problems of the country (Fortuna & Lennett, 1987, p. 16). So Congress revised the law to provide great detail and specificity to close loopholes and expand the RCRA's application. In the 1984 Amendments, Congress explicitly sought to discourage the continued use of landfills for disposing of hazardous wastes and to encourage source reduction, recycling, and treatment of hazardous wastes.

Subsequently, Congress passed the Superfund Amendments and Reauthorization Act of 1986 (SARA), which, as the title implies, reauthorized EPA to identify and take action on hazardous waste sites. The Act also required that EPA set clear standards in its regulations as to who is responsible for site cleanup, how clean the site has to be, and how to select the technological method to clean up the site. Part of what motivated Congress' call for such clear standards was the growing recognition that in implementing site cleanups, many problems were actually made worse. As a result, the growing body of case law on the liability established by the Superfund Act suggests that it is becoming increasingly difficult for corporate officials and employees to avoid responsibility for illegal disposal of hazardous substances. The law allows individuals and corporations to be held criminally liable, even if they themselves did not commit the act of illegal disposal.

SARA also contained provisions that require each state to assure the availability of adequate hazardous waste treatment and disposal facilities to handle that state's expected hazardous wastes for the next 20 years, which, in effect, requires each state to project for the next 20 years how much hazardous waste will likely be produced there. Then it required that the state demonstrate that it has or will have the capacity to properly treat and/or dispose of this projected volume. States cannot simply propose to transport such wastes to another state unless they can provide documentation, and unless the state to which wastes are being transported has excess capacity to handle it. SARA authorized the EPA to withhold Superfund cleanup money from any state that did not provide such assurances by October 1989. The logic of this "capacity assurance" provision is simply that the federal government should not have to pay the bill for cleaning up hazardous waste sites in states where there has been no effort to avoid creating such sites in the first place. Thus, Congress tried to break a never-ending cycle of creation and cleanup of waste sites, all paid for out of the federal treasury.

SARA also required that the EPA, along with the Department of Health and Human Services and the Agency for Toxic Substances and Disease Registry, prepare a priority list of hazardous substances to be regulated under Superfund. This list was to contain the hazardous chemicals most commonly found at hazardous waste sites on the National Priority List, and which pose the most significant threats to human health. The EPA and cooperating agencies published the first list of some 100 such substances in 1987, and in 1991 added to it substances listed as priorities under the Safe Drinking Water Act Amendments of 1988 (discussed in Chapter 4). Consequently, the EPA was able to satisfy the requirements of several pieces of legislation by developing overlapping lists.

There has been other recent legislation specifically aimed at preventing certain types of solid or hazardous waste disposal, such as the 1989 ban on dumping hazardous medical waste into oceans and the Great Lakes, a practice that led to such wastes washing up on many beaches in the middle of the summer. However, RCRA and the 1984 Hazardous and Solid Waste Amendments, TSCA, CERCLA, and SARA form the core of hazardous waste regulation legislation.

Regulation of environmentally damaging agricultural chemicals, especially pesticides, insecticides, and fungicides, has been largely the product of several additional pieces of legislation. In 1972 Congress passed the Federal Environmental Pesticide Control Act. This legislation provided the EPA and the Department of Agriculture with a range of regulatory responsibilities and options not available under the then-operative Federal Insecticide, Fungicide, and Rodenticide Act of 1947. By the early 1970s, nearly everyone was greatly dissatisfied with the existing law.

Much of this dissatisfaction grew out of efforts to regulate the use and abuse of DDT, the pesticide given so much notoriety by Rachel

Carson. As noted in Chapter 2, the Nixon administration had announced in 1969 a phaseout of the use of DDT in agriculture. Extending this, the Secretary of Agriculture announced a ban on all but essential uses of DDT by late 1971. What became clear to many, however, was that the existing law required this ban to be applied to specific uses and not to the chemical itself. Thus, DDT was still available on the market, although with a label specifying the uses for which it was banned, and there was apparently no additional effort to enforce the ban (Bosso, 1987, p. 155). Partly in recognition of the need to avoid future problems with hazardous chemicals used as agricultural pesticides, Congress embarked on specific efforts to provide the legal authority for the banning of such chemicals themselves. This legislation was amended in 1978.

The 1972 Federal Environmental Pesticide Control Act gave the EPA substantially more authority to regulate pesticides than any federal agency had previously. It required that producers of pesticides register their chemicals with the EPA, which could reject an application for a chemical if it found that the product posed "unreasonable adverse effects on the environment," and also required that the applicant provide fairly detailed data in support of the application. Registrants were allowed to withhold some information if they could argue that it constituted a trade secret. Information about possible health effects from exposure to chemicals, also a required part of the application process, could be available for public scrutiny. Anyone outside of the EPA who objected to registration based on health effects information could not stop the registration; they could only petition the EPA to begin a process to consider revoking the already issued registration. Finally, it created civil judicial standing for people who might have been adversely affected by exposure to the chemical, so that they could seek compensation from the manufacturer or user. The 1978 Amendments, as will be described later, weakened many aspects of the EPA's statutory authority regulating pesticides.

The Policy-Making Processes
in Federal Hazardous Waste Management

The review of the recent history of legislation enacted to help protect people and the environment from hazardous and toxic wastes reveals little about how these acts came to be. Looking at their policy-making processes will show how several major clashes of values, represented in a vast array of disparate political interests, were able to be momentarily resolved in creating the legislation. An investigation into the implementation processes will provide much greater detail on what the various pieces of legislation really mean—how they are specifically translated into governmental action.

Making Hazardous Waste Policy:
From RCRA to HSWA, From CERCLA to SARA

Federal hazardous waste policy-making is probably best viewed as something of a continuous process, probably starting in the early 1970s. To understand the enactment of the Hazardous and Solid Waste Amendments of 1984, for example, one must understand what happened in the enactment and implementation of RCRA. To understand the adoption of SARA, it is extremely helpful to know how CERCLA was enacted and implemented. The course of events represents a sort of trial-and-error process in which Congress tries to accomplish some goals, the goals cannot be or are not achieved, and Congress tries again.

Hazardous Waste Problem Formation and Policy Formulation

The events surrounding the effort to revise and improve RCRA constitute what Barke (1988) refers to as "rational policy learning." The policy-making process was a straightforward collection of activities guided by common recognition of the problems with RCRA and how these problems should be corrected. By the mid-1980s, a variety of information pointed strongly to the conclusion that RCRA implementation was problematic. As already noted, considerable concern arose over the Reagan EPA's commitment to hazardous waste regulation, and many in Congress concluded that new, more specific, detailed legislation would be necessary to get EPA to focus concerted attention in this area. Some have suggested that the EPA's effort on RCRA was more one of benign neglect and crisis management than one of dedicated implementation. Others, including Senator George Mitchell (D-Maine), a principal sponsor of the eventual Senate version of a revised law, stated very clearly why he felt new legislation was needed:

It has become evident that a strong congressional expression of disapproval of EPA's slow and timid implementation of the existing law is

necessary. . . . EPA has not implemented the RCRA aggressively. The
Agency has missed deadlines, proposed inadequate regulations, and even
exacerbated the hazardous waste problem by suspending certain regulations. . . . This is not acceptable. (Fortuna & Lennett, 1987, p. 8)

While some blamed the EPA for the problems of RCRA, others came
to independent conclusions that RCRA simply failed to provide a clear
statement of the philosophy to guide hazardous waste management.
RCRA left too many questions open to interpretation, which almost
guaranteed that there would be implementation problems. For example,
RCRA authorized the EPA to issue regulations "as may be necessary to
protect human health and the environment." This vague language,
combined with no language addressing issues such as whether very
small hazardous waste producers should be treated differently from
very large ones, whether recycled wastes should be treated differently,
or whether there should be specific limits on the amounts and types of
hazardous wastes disposed of in landfills, all made it very likely that
problems would arise (Fortuna & Lennett, pp. 8-9).

By 1984 there seemed to have been agreement among everyone,
except perhaps the Reagan administration, that RCRA needed to be
reformed. Support coalesced around passage of legislation that eventually was called the Hazardous and Solid Waste Amendments of 1984.
Members of Congress, state regulatory agencies, environmental interest
groups, and the trade and industry associations representing the regulated industries all expressed the desire to improve federal hazardous
waste legislation (Fortuna & Lennett, pp. 14-15). Perhaps more than in
any other environmental area, there seemed to be consensus that hazardous waste legislation should be changed to clarify goals, to specify
EPA actions, and to strengthen enforcement. At the initiative of James
Florio (D-New Jersey), the House version and the final law carried
explicit language specifying what would happen (i.e., what the law
would be) if the EPA failed to issue regulations as directed (Barke,
1988, p. 156). With very little opposition, the Hazardous and Solid
Waste Amendments Act passed easily.

The sequences of events surrounding the passage of CERCLA and
SARA exhibit similarities with RCRA and its amendments, but there
are some unique aspects as well. By the late 1970s, it was clear that
existing legislation did not permit the federal government to take
actions to help clean up hazardous waste sites. For one thing, there was
no clear financing mechanism. For another, RCRA was directed toward

upgrading operating disposal facilities, not abandoned or closed ones. And in many lawsuits brought by the EPA against parties it felt were responsible, under RCRA the courts interpreted the liability quite narrowly. Very often waste generators were able to avoid paying for cleanups by shifting liability to someone else. For example, when a waste generator contracted with a waste hauler to transport its wastes somewhere else, the courts held that the liability had been transferred as well (Grunbaum, 1988, pp. 164-165). When the EPA tried to hold the hauler liable, often the hauler would declare bankruptcy and avoid financial responsibility. Thus, government would have to pay the entire cost of cleanup, which is typically not an insignificant amount of money.

Added to this recognition was the fact that Ronald Reagan had just been elected President. Fearing that the Reagan administration would take little initiative on hazardous waste cleanup, many proponents of a clearer and stronger piece of legislation pushed to enact a law before the end of 1980. There had been a number of legislative proposals introduced in Congress during 1980, including one by the Carter administration, and House and Senate versions. Bowman (1988) suggests that CERCLA was adopted in a rush to accomplish something in the area of hazardous waste cleanup before a new, less pro-cleanup Congress and presidential administration took office. This may well explain, in part, why much of CERCLA's language was less explicit than it could have been.

Hazardous Waste Policy
Implementation and Enforcement

Implementation of RCRA in its first few years was less than impressive. The problems of implementation should perhaps be placed in the context of the times. When RCRA was passed by Congress, it included very broad language directing the EPA to issue regulations concerning which wastes would be subjected to federal regulation, the standards for generators of hazardous wastes to receive permits, and the details of the "cradle to grave" provisions. There was scarcely any information available to anyone about how serious a problem hazardous waste really was. Indeed, part of the rationale for RCRA was that it would help create an extensive range of information about how much hazardous waste was being produced, transported, and disposed of. Apparently, hazardous waste regulation was not a very high priority for the Carter administration, since it consistently underfunded the EPA's efforts, and the EPA consistently missed deadlines specified in the legislation (Fortuna & Lennett, pp. 10-11).

In 1978 a number of environmental organizations, including the Environmental Defense Fund, filed a federal lawsuit against the EPA to force it to comply with the schedule expressed by Congress. The court ordered the EPA to provide an estimate of when such rules would be issued, and then ordered the EPA to comply with its own schedule. When the EPA missed this set of deadlines, it offered a revised schedule, which it largely met. However, there were still a number of important regulations that EPA had not issued by 1981. These included the standards by which landfills would be able to apply for, and receive, permits to accept hazardous wastes, and standards governing underground storage tanks containing hazardous wastes. Many of the regulations that were issued had major omissions or exemptions; facilities that burned hazardous wastes to produce energy were exempted from the permitting process. The early record of RCRA implementation certainly appeared to be one of benign neglect.

This benign neglect of hazardous waste regulation soon became transformed into hostility as the Reagan administration got under way (Portney, 1984). Paralleling implementation experiences with other environmental regulations, the Reagan administration brought with it absolutely no commitment to environmental protection. Indeed, in planning for the new administration even before Reagan's inauguration, David Stockman (who later became Reagan's Director of the Office of Management and Budget, or OMB) revealed a plan to rescind, revise, or defer many of RCRA's provisions. The principal vehicle for this was the Executive Order requiring all federal regulations to be approved by OMB; and the Task Force, headed by Vice-President George Bush, listed RCRA provisions among those that OMB would not approve because of the burdens they placed on the private sector (Fortuna & Lennett, p. 12).

In terms of actual implementation of RCRA, it was not long before the EPA, under Ann Gorsuch, began to retreat from what little regulatory effort had already been accomplished. For example, in mid-1981, Gorsuch notified OMB that the EPA would essentially suspend the rules already issued governing existing incinerators and surface hazardous waste storage impoundment areas. In late 1981 the EPA announced that it would defer or eliminate already-issued financial responsibility regulations. In early 1982 the EPA postponed record-keeping and reporting requirements, eliminated the required assessment of groundwater around areas found to be contaminated by hazardous wastes, and removed the ban on landfill disposal of containerized liquid hazardous wastes. The EPA postponed and delayed issuing new regulations. Eventually, under court order, the EPA issued standards governing the granting of permits to hazardous waste disposal facilities, but subsequently took little action to actually grant such permits to operating facilities. By late 1984 only 5 landfill facilities and 17 incinerators in the entire nation had received RCRA permits (Fortuna & Lennett, p. 13). Enforcement of existing regulations was minimal, and the EPA often did nothing to try to ensure that hazardous waste facilities were operated according to permits. This, of course, set the stage for enactment of the Hazardous and Solid Waste Amendments of 1984, Congress' legislative response to the EPA's progress in implementing RCRA.

Many of the same problems characterized implementation of CERCLA. A key portion of the Superfund program was the identification and assessment of contaminated sites around the country to determine whether they deserved to be included on the National Priorities List. By 1982 the EPA had worked with the states and conducted its first round of identification and had issued its first priorities list. By 1987 the list contained some 964 sites, including 98 in New Jersey, 64 in Michigan, 60 in California, and 59 each in Pennsylvania and New York.

The National Priorities List was created through the development of a hazard ranking system. When a state recommended sites for inclusion on the list, the EPA scored each site that could potentially be included according to the quantity and type of hazardous waste present, how close the site was to population centers or sensitive environments, and the potential and actual migratory routes through which the pollution could cause serious health effects—groundwater, surface water, or air. Sites that received a higher hazard ranking would receive a higher priority on the list, and higher priority sites would qualify for Superfund cleanup funds. Creating this list was no small or inexpensive task. Simply trying to determine what kinds of pollutants might be buried on a given site can take years to complete.

The process used in creating the priorities listing was itself criticized on a number of grounds. The U.S. Office of Technology Assessment issued a report containing such a criticism in 1985. This report noted that the methods used to score the sites were biased and produced inconsistent results. For example, it suggested that the way hazard rankings were affected by the score for the migratory route might not produce accurate assessments. If there were two sites that contained comparable types and amounts of hazardous wastes, but had different migration routes (air, groundwater, surface water), the resulting ranking might not reflect the actual hazard posed. One site that received a high score for being close to an underground aquifer and was not near a lake or did not pose an air pollution problem might receive a lower overall ranking than the other site, which received only moderate scores on all three migration routes (Bowman, 1988, p. 133).

The problems with Superfund implementation became compounded in the first 2 or 3 years of the Reagan administration because of what might be called the "politicization" of the EPA. To begin with, Ann Gorsuch was not particularly committed to the role of the federal government in environmental policy, and the administrator of the hazardous waste division, Rita Lavelle, had no prior experience with hazardous waste issues. Additionally, the strategy of the Reagan EPA under Gorsuch was philosophically opposed to strict enforcement. Instead, the EPA preferred to follow a nonconfrontational approach, where the EPA would negotiate with responsible parties to settle claims without going through judicial proceedings. And there is evidence that key political appointees in the EPA had been working with the chemical industry to relax rules and enforcement so that specific chemical companies would benefit (Cohen 1984, pp. 280-281). The top management of the EPA discouraged civil servants from serious enforcement of Superfund, creating an atmosphere where many EPA employees felt that they served two diametrically opposed masters (Palumbo & Maynard-Moody, 307-308).

The problems at EPA got even worse when Gorsuch demanded the resignation of Lavelle for going over her head to Edwin Meese, counsel to President Reagan. When Lavelle refused to resign, she was fired by the President in February 1983. Amidst all these events, Congress held oversight hearings in an effort to determine whether Superfund and other hazardous waste programs were being implemented as intended. Career civil servants in the EPA went directly to congressional committees as "whistleblowers" to report that top EPA officials were circumventing the law. When Gorsuch and Lavelle claimed executive privilege and refused to provide Congress with the EPA's hazardous waste enforcement files, Congress cited them for contempt. By March 1983 Gorsuch resigned under pressure, and was replaced by William Ruckelshaus, who had also been the first EPA administrator. Eventually, four top EPA political appointees were forced to resign, and Lavelle was convicted of criminal acts (Rohr, 1988, p. 171).

Together these events made implementing Superfund difficult and ineffective. Very little progress was made toward actually cleaning up hazardous wastes, and little was done to recover the costs of cleanups. Indeed, one of the practices that received much criticism was the negotiated settlement with potentially responsible parties. The problem was that, in many cases, the EPA would negotiate and settle cases before the costs of cleanup were known. Thus, the EPA would claim that it was able to recover a certain amount of money, but frequently that amount was only a small fraction of what was needed to clean up the site in question. Since that time, however, the Superfund program has been re-energized, partly by a combination of new personnel and new and specific directions from Congress in the Superfund Amendments and Reauthorization Act of 1986 (SARA).

In addition to the priorities list of Superfund sites, the EPA is engaged in determining what kinds of actions are necessary for particular sites. Site assessments include determining what kind of remedial action is necessary and creating plans for the necessary action. Sometimes the plans call for the containment of hazardous wastes, especially underground wastes, so that they will not leak and contaminate water sources. In other cases, the plans might call for the excavation of soil and other material and transporting these wastes to another, less-hazardous location, usually a "secure" landfill. Sometimes the soil is incinerated at very high temperatures, and what remains after incineration may also be placed in a secure landfill. When cleanup involves removal of material from a waterway, the same processes are often used.

Controversies often arise over what level of cleanup is necessary for a given site. Since responsible parties are liable for cleanup costs, they frequently challenge EPA cleanup assessments and plans, arguing that the site in question needs less-expensive remediation than the EPA claims. For example, an assessment might require the excavation and removal of contaminated soil, usually a more expensive alternative than containing the hazardous material in place. The responsible party might claim that containment is sufficient for this particular site. However, the current law allows EPA to essentially impose its cleanup plan on parties, proceed to clean up the site accordingly, and try to recover the costs later.

Making Public Policy Toward Pesticides

The federal regulation of pesticides, as noted earlier, has taken place largely through enactment and implementation of two major pieces of legislation, the Federal Environmental Pesticide Control Act of 1972, and the 1978 Amendments to this Act. Experiences with pesticide regulation have been somewhat different from those surrounding hazardous waste issues.

Problem Formation and Policy Formulation

Earlier it was noted that the 1972 Pesticide Control Act was, at least in part, motivated by recognition of the difficulties that arose in efforts to ban DDT. Bosso (1987), in his extensive analysis of the processes of enacting both the 1972 and 1978 legislation, paints a picture where reform of the laws governing pesticide regulation had to overcome significant and entrenched interests supporting the lack of government involvement. He suggests that major agricultural interests, the manufacturers of chemical pesticides, and congressional committees had worked for years to ensure that pesticide and insecticide use would continue. The scientific development of pesticides and insecticides ushered in what Bosso calls the "pesticides paradigm." The driving force behind this was the central belief that increased agricultural production required chemical use. In a sense, the attitudes of the pro-pesticide interests embody the rearguard values toward the role of nature in society, as delineated in Chapter 1. These interests believed that new agricultural chemicals provided them with the vehicle for people to dominate over nature. It hurt not at all that pesticides promised to convert agriculture from an economic backwater to an economic growth industry.

To a large degree, efforts to reform pesticide regulation were ushered in by the same series of events that brought the Clean Air Act of 1970 and the Clean Water Act of 1972. What led to congressional action was the simultaneous emergence of environmental interest groups to oppose agricultural and chemical interest groups, and the rise of general public opinion in support of environmental protection. However, the path to legislative change was not as smooth or as clear-cut as that found in the other environmental reforms of the times. As Bosso (p. 161) states:

> To deal with air or water pollution was one thing—since those battles pitted an aroused public against a rather shaky opposition—but to deal with pesticides was to run into a heavily complex, less public issue and against a well-organized, powerfully entrenched configuration of policy specialists.

The result for pesticide policy reform was that the process was slow; literally hundreds of proposals were made for reform, including proposals from the Nixon administration and EPA; and dozens of pieces of legislation were introduced into Congress—some to control pesticides, some in an effort to prevent control of pesticides. Although actions in the House of Representatives were in the domain of the Agriculture committee, the Senate Agriculture and Commerce committees shared jurisdiction. All of these factors contributed to an unusually complex policy-making process and created a very complicated array of issues that had to be sorted out. One of the major issues was the pro-pesticide proposal to indemnify the makers and users of pesticides. According to this proposal, if a pesticide already in use were banned, the federal government would have to reimburse not only the pesticide producers but also the farmers who owned pesticide products for their financial loss. This was an extremely controversial proposal, one which deeply angered environmentalists and some members of Congress (Bosso, p. 175).

The result of this process was the adoption of the 1972 Act, which gave EPA new powers to regulate pesticides. It provided stronger chemical registration requirements and gave the EPA authority to determine what would have to be included in applications for registration. It also provided much stricter controls of the manufacture and use of chemicals, which had to be explicitly stated on chemical products' labels. And anyone adversely affected by chemical use would have a clear route to judicial redress.

By the time the 1972 Act came up for reauthorization in 1977, many issues had arisen about the effectiveness of the earlier law in protecting people from exposure to pesticides. To begin with, a number of major incidents highlighted the inability of the existing law to prohibit or stop unsafe handling of pesticides. In addition, the EPA was seriously backlogged in reviewing and issuing registrations for new pesticides. To make matters worse, those registrations granted by the EPA were apparently decided without any pretense of using complete information or systematic review (Bosso, p. 199). Numerous incidents revealed that the EPA had approved registration of pesticides which contained ingredients, unknown to the EPA, that had already been banned. For example, the EPA approved registration of the chemical Mirex, used widely in the fight against the well-publicized onslaught of fire ants in the South, even though Mirex contained the already banned chemical Kepone. EPA banned Mirex in late 1978, which infuriated many southern members of Congress, but the way the process of registration operated made clear the need for revised legislation.

In the process of amending the pesticides Act, it became clear that many of the interests associated with the opposition to the 1972 legislation were alive and well. Indeed, many of those opposing regulation of pesticides had actually become stronger. By 1978 the deregulatory ethos was already evident, and Congress eventually enacted a revised law, which backed away from stricter regulation of pesticide chemicals. The 1978 Amendments changed registration and re-registration procedures and provided the EPA with the authority to issue conditional registrations, even if insufficient information were available for full registration. Thus, Congress approved the possible registration of potentially unsafe pesticides. It also provided for an expanded role for state agencies to enforce the use of agricultural pesticides, rather than have this role performed by an overburdened federal EPA. It also allowed state agencies to tailor federal regulations to local needs as long as the overall state enforcement program was acceptable to the EPA. Thus, much decision-making on pesticide regulation was delegated to the states.

State and Local Governments in Hazardous Waste Management

While most of the discussion of hazardous waste policy has focused on the federal government, state and local governments have not been inactive or unimportant in hazardous waste management (Lester, Franke, Bowman, & Kramer, 1983). Many states have been very aggressive on issues of hazardous wastes, working to clean up existing threats and to prevent future threats from occurring. States have also been left holding the bag, so to speak, for making some aspects of federal waste management work (Kamlet, 1979).

In recent years, a number of states have adopted fairly aggressive programs of hazardous waste management. Not all states have been particularly interested in regulating the production, storage, and disposal of hazardous wastes, and in many cases, the EPA has not fully delegated responsibility for waste management because of the lack of an acceptable state implementation plan. Typically, state governments have had to confront a variety of problems in designing their hazardous waste management policies and procedures. For example, as the state role in hazardous waste regulation has gradually increased, responsibility for implementing and enforcing regulations has sometimes become fragmented. In some states, responsibility for different aspects of regulation is delegated to a variety of different state, regional, or local agencies. This fragmented approach not infrequently leads to difficulties in coordination among the various agencies, and often makes compliance difficult for parties who are the targets of regulation.

There are a number of ways that states have become aggressive in hazardous waste management. Some states, such as Georgia, Massachusetts, New York, and Oregon, have tried to overcome problems of fragmentation by creating large single agencies that implement nearly every aspect of hazardous waste policy. Other states have simply adopted mandatory hazardous waste management procedures that are more stringent than those required by federal law. For example, California, New York, and Massachusetts regulate hazardous waste storage to permit smaller quantities to be stored for shorter periods of time than allowed by the EPA. Michigan, New York, and Oregon rely on a more stringent hazardous waste manifest system, requiring manifests for more substances and in smaller amounts than federal law. Finally, New Jersey and Oregon have invested heavily in recycling options to reduce the volume of hazardous and solid wastes needing to be disposed of (Jessup, 1988, pp. 67, 223-224, 237-238, 335, 386).

Perhaps the greatest problem with state efforts at regulating hazardous wastes is the lack of resources. Federal laws and their implementation place substantial compliance responsibility in the hands of the states, and very often do not provide much in the way of resources to help support this increased responsibility. State governments must weigh responding to what is sometimes simply perceived as federal pressure, compared to responding to various other demands on state government. The politics of hazardous waste management in the states may be quite varied, and very different from the federal experience. In a particular state, if a polluting industry happens to be highly concentrated and makes large contributions to the state's economy, that industry may be able to exercise extreme influence over the shape and commitment of the state to hazardous waste issues. Indeed, although there is little evidence that this is actually the case, many state government officials believe that strict hazardous waste regulations place their states at a major competitive disadvantage. In the face of these constraints, it is perhaps remarkable that states have been able to accomplish as much as they have.

Intergovernmental Tensions

Although many states do in fact have well-developed hazardous waste management functions, these functions are necessarily performed within the context of the federal system. Perhaps not unlike other environmental policy areas discussed in previous chapters, hazardous waste policy administration has involved many joint efforts between federal and state agencies. In this process, especially in the context of specific site cleanup efforts, differences of strategy or philosophy can sometimes create tensions among officials from different levels of government or with private sector parties (Zimmerman, 1988). In a detailed analysis of the patterns of tensions that developed in the process of trying to clean up four sites in South Carolina, Bowman (1984) discovered a number of different kinds of tensions. EPA involvement typically does not start with the discovery of a hazardous waste site. Usually, the site has been located and identified by a state agency, and it is not uncommon that the state involvement was initiated by a local agency that first became aware of the site. Before the EPA ever becomes involved, there is often some form of tension between state and local officials, frequently over who will take responsibility and pay for site cleanup. Thus, tensions sometimes involve clashes over which level of government is, or should be, responsible for hazardous waste site cleanup.

EPA involvement in site cleanup becomes imposed on existing intergovernmental tensions. When the EPA becomes involved, it usually is accompanied by high expectations that the federal government will finance the cleanup, sparing the local and state agencies the expense. Frequently, these expectations are dashed when the EPA cannot or will not finance the cleanup. Not all tension is created over issues of finance. Sometimes dissatisfaction with progress by one party will cause relations with the others to become strained. For example, local officials might become disenchanted if the EPA halts cleanup in order to facilitate recovery of costs from a responsible producer of the hazardous wastes (Bowman, 1984, p. 239). However, cleaning up sites is not the only source of state and local controversy in hazardous waste regulation.

**Siting Hazardous Waste Facilities
and the NIMBY Syndrome**

One of the consequences of federal legislation for hazardous waste management has been increased pressure on states to find safe ways of disposing of hazardous wastes. For the most part, this requires the siting and construction of disposal facilities (secure landfills) and treatment facilities, including high-temperature incinerators to burn wastes. This pressure is the result of many features of the federal legislation, including the requirement that states provide "capacity assurance" for the next 20 years, and that hazardous wastes be tracked from the time of their creation until final disposal. Despite this pressure, there has been a marked decrease in the number of places for hazardous waste disposal. Old facilities have been closed or taken out of service, often because they cannot meet the stringent federal standards and are therefore considered a significant health threat, and new facilities have not been sited.

It has become extremely difficult to site new facilities, largely because of local opposition. Efforts to site hazardous waste facilities are among some of the most heated and controversial of all political events (Andrews, 1988). A party proposing to site a hazardous waste facility today is likely to meet significant local opposition, and this opposition is overwhelmingly effective in preventing such facilities from actually being constructed. It is probably possible to count on one hand the number of new facilities successfully sited in the United States over the past 10 years. The local opposition to facility siting and construction is frequently referred to as being motivated by the NIMBY, or Not-In-My-Back-Yard, Syndrome (Portney, 1991a).

The NIMBY Syndrome, as a concept, describes people who accept the idea that such facilities have to be sited somewhere, but who simply refuse to have them sited in their towns or neighborhoods. For example, with respect to siting hazardous waste treatment facilities, survey research indicates that only about one-fourth of the people in the United States oppose the idea of relying on treatment facilities somewhere in their respective states, but as many as two-thirds refuse to have these facilities sited in their respective communities (Portney, 1991a, pp. 12-13). Ironically, local opposition to hazardous waste facility siting may potentially make the problems of hazardous waste worse. When local generators of hazardous wastes have fewer and fewer places to safely dispose of their materials, and when the costs of such disposal keep rising, this creates a major incentive for them to seek unsafe and illegal disposal options.

Siting efforts often embody a clash of values over the role of government in society, particularly the clash between individualism and communitarianism. The company seeking to site a treatment facility frequently asserts the right to do so as an extension of ownership of the property on which the proposed site would be built. Sometimes such developers refuse to acknowledge that any government agency—federal, state, or local—has any right to prevent the facility from being built. Local residents, however, adopt opposite positions very clearly based on communitarian values. Such a position argues that the developer should not be allowed to site the facility if it poses a threat to community health and welfare. After all, there is no way to guarantee that treatment facilities will be absolutely safe. This clash of values is typically settled through the practical reality that the local community is able to exercise the political influence to prevent administrative approval. The NIMBY Syndrome usually prevails.

Many states seem to have decided that local communitarian values have gone too far, and that there are other communitarian values at stake. Siting hazardous waste facilities may well provide benefits to a larger community of people. Consequently, most states have tried enacting laws that would overcome the NIMBY Syndrome, but none has found a magic answer. States have pursued policies that try to take away local decision-making by preempting local authority. These efforts have generally failed, leading some researchers to declare that preemption does not actually occur, and is therefore a myth (Morell & Magorian, 1982).

States have tried overcoming local opposition by involving the affected community in the decision process from nearly the beginning, bringing in expert consultants in negotiation and mediation, and offering economic compensation designed to create incentives for local residents to accept facilities. Parties proposing to build hazardous waste facilities have been known to offer paying everyone's local property tax bill for a long period of time, and to even give them life insurance policies. Developers have also proposed giving "host communities" new police and fire equipment, repaving streets, hiring a large number of local residents, providing college scholarships to needy students, and many other incentives. However, no method has yet been found to make initially unacceptable facilities palatable. Sometimes people in a potential host community become outraged at these offers, feeling that the developer is simply trying to bribe people into dropping their opposition (Portney, 1991a, pp. 23-48).

The inability to site new facilities, coupled with the loss of existing facilities, has created a significant dilemma for the states, and for waste management policy in general. States do not wish to fail to comply with federal regulations, and they certainly do not want to see hazardous wastes produced in their jurisdictions disposed of improperly or illegally. Yet there is little state regulators or policymakers can do without completely stifling economic activity and development. Until workable solutions expand the actual capacity to safely dispose of hazardous wastes, it will be very difficult for public policy to make real progress toward protecting people from exposure to hazardous wastes and preventing future Superfund sites from being created.

Controversies in Hazardous Waste Policy: A Summary

The history of legislation and implementation experiences with hazardous waste management and policy may be less lengthy than that found in other environmental areas, but it certainly has not been lacking in controversy. Federal involvement started with efforts to tighten up existing practices in the handling of hazardous wastes, including their disposal, with an eye toward minimizing the creation of future hazardous waste sites. It also included efforts to undo many of the errors of the past by providing a fund to help finance the cleanup of existing sites. Subsequently, federal efforts have focused on creating incentives for source reduction—to make sure that the volume of hazardous materials finding their way into the environment is reduced—by encouraging private industry to seek alternatives to the production of hazardous wastes, and by encouraging the recycling and recovery, rather than disposal, of hazardous materials. And it has worked toward guaranteeing that remaining hazardous wastes are handled safely and disposed of in ways that pose the least possible risk to people's health and welfare.

These well-intended strategies have run headlong into difficulties from a variety of sources. Perhaps foremost among these have been presidential administrations less than fully enthusiastic about broad-based implementation. Certainly under the Reagan administration of 1981 to 1983, there is clear evidence that the EPA did not wish to implement hazardous waste policies in an aggressive, pro-environment way. But this has not been the only difficulty faced by hazardous waste policy.

Perhaps more than in any other area of environmental policy, Congress has explicitly sought to push a recalcitrant agency, the EPA, into taking its legislation seriously. It has done this by performing serious oversight of the EPA's operations and, when necessary, has revised legislation to require the EPA to take very specific actions. Earlier hazardous waste legislation called for the EPA to prepare lists of possible hazardous substances, but when the EPA put little effort into this task, Congress produced specific numbers of hazardous substances to be evaluated for possible regulation. When the EPA continued to allow landfills, including unsecured landfills, to be used to dispose of hazardous wastes, Congress enacted legislation explicitly prohibiting this practice. When the EPA failed to take much action toward licensing landfills for hazardous waste disposal, Congress enacted explicit legislation to force this issue.

But EPA inactivity has not been the only problem. In some cases, the initial intent of Congress was not fulfilled because the earlier legislation was ill-conceived. The intent to improve the quality of the environment by providing funds for hazardous waste site cleanup did not always work. In some cases, efforts to clean up hazardous waste sites actually made the problems worse. Consequently, Congress has tried to rectify this problem by requiring the EPA to be aggressive in specifying what techniques are required to clean up specific sites, and what kinds of actions would be necessary to make sure that a particular site is actually "clean."

In efforts to regulate pesticides, the record is less clear. Perhaps starting with the fact that Congress itself has had a much more difficult time agreeing on what the nation's pesticide regulation policy ought to be, major pesticide users and producers have largely been able to prevent more aggressive regulation. Earlier efforts at stricter regulation in the 1970s were not effective, and subsequently these efforts have been replaced by retrenchment. This is not to say that pesticides are unregulated. However, many of the ways that people could be protected by federal policy from the harmful effects of pesticide exposure have not been pursued.

Tensions among federal, state, and local levels of government, and between government and the private sector, have also contributed to hazardous waste policy difficulties. Involvement of the EPA in specific hazardous waste cleanups sometimes creates tensions with state or local officials also involved. Frequently, state and local officials want cleanup to occur more quickly, while the EPA sometimes must balance the cleanup with its desire to recover costs of cleanup through legal channels. In its efforts to make sure that sites are cleaned up properly, the

EPA may impose cleanup requirements on private sector parties that are viewed as unnecessary and overly expensive.

All of the efforts to improve hazardous waste management have increased the need to find safe places and processes for hazardous waste disposal. But the politics of state and local hazardous waste facility siting, frequently characterized by the NIMBY Syndrome, has made complying with federal regulations very difficult. For example, to comply with the EPA's 20-year capacity assurance requirements for disposing of hazardous wastes, states have had to plan on increased numbers of facilities. But, at least to date, the lack of success in actually siting these facilities raises serious questions about the value of many capacity assurance plans. Unless some way is found to improve the success of facility siting, this could end up being another case of missed deadlines in a well-intended policy.

6

Controversies in Environmental
Policy—Past, Present, and Future
A Brief Epilogue

The previous chapters reviewed a variety of both current and historical controversies in public environmental policy. Controversies in specific environmental areas tend to reveal a general pattern, where disagreements were rooted in clashes of values, often represented in the public policy-making process. Most controversies in environmental policy are rooted in clashes of values involving science and technology versus humanism, economic efficiency versus humanism, the role of nature in society, and the role of government in society. All of these value clashes have found their way into the policy-making process and typically pit the values of science, technology, and economics against the practice of politics. The events that are characteristic parts of the processes of environmental problem formation, policy formulation, policy legitimation and adoption, implementation, and evaluation, have all been influenced by these values.

In addition to these recurring clashes, environmental policy controversies include some issues that are periodically revisited. Federal efforts to improve the quality of the environment, whether in the air, water, or ground, always seem to start with primary emphasis on state and local government responsibility. Each policy area also experiences some degree of frustration over this primary emphasis, largely because state and local governments have not been able to make significant progress toward environmental improvement. Such governments sometimes feel the need to respond to economic pressures—to not interfere with economic development and the creation of jobs—while others might not have the resources to take aggressive environmental action. Even when some states do become more directly involved and aggressive in environmental protection, the problems of pollution they try to address are not always amenable to localized action. As noted earlier, some states tried to take aggressive action against acid rain, yet because the states experiencing the effects of acid rain are typically not the same states where acid rain-causing pollution is emitted, any individual state's efforts might well be constrained.

At the same time, however, the brief history of federal environmental policy also reveals that extremely ambitious environmental policy may not be any more effective than reliance on state and local governments. Policies that set deadlines for compliance with pollution limits requiring the development and use of technologies not yet in existence, as occurred in air and water policy, may not have produced a cleaner environment than might otherwise have been achieved.

These historical issues are by no means relegated to the past. Many of these same issues will likely recur in the future. As the federal budget deficit requires federal policymakers to pursue options for cutting spending, federal effort will probably not be able to keep pace with the discovery of new environmental problems. Pursuit of these options may well place greater responsibility for environmental protection into the hands of the states, but with much less federal financial and technical assistance to state and local governments than in earlier periods. In short, fiscal and political realities may once again place the principal responsibility for environmental protection in the domain of state and local governments.

Expectations about future technologies and the role that such technologies should play in public policy responses will continue to be problematic. For example, interest groups in a number of states have sought to decrease the volume of plastic trash being placed in landfills by banning certain types of product packaging, especially packaging that is not recyclable. Part of the justification for such a ban is that it would encourage packaging manufacturers to develop new methods and new materials for packaging that would be easier to recycle, or would be more biodegradable if disposed of in landfills. However, these packaging products, and sometimes the technologies to make them, do not yet exist. Requiring the development of such materials might not be any more effective in promoting a clean environment than was requiring nonexistent technologies to clean up the air. Even if such new packaging is eventually developed, it is not likely to meet the deadlines imposed by well-meaning public policy.

Other local environmental issues will continue to be controversial, especially the siting of hazardous waste treatment and disposal facilities. Public policies attempting to improve the handling and management of hazardous wastes require the increased use of safe disposal options. However, public willingness to live anywhere near facilities providing these safe options is nonexistent. Efforts to site facilities will continue to engender intense public opposition, calling into question policies that require waste treatment. Unless new, more-effective siting methods can be found, the lack of treatment options for producers of hazardous wastes will be a serious problem for some time to come.

While this book discussed a variety of environmental policy controversies, there are many others that were either not mentioned or were discussed only briefly. Some of these are issues still of significant importance today. A few examples of some important issues not discussed might provide the basis for independent investigation.

Little mention was made of federal policy toward endangered species, although controversies still arise over these issues. Debates and controversies still occur over whether it is a worthwhile goal of federal or state policy to try to save endangered species at the possible expense of jobs and economic development. Not too long ago, for example, efforts to begin cutting down old-growth forests for timber in the Pacific Northwest were opposed by environmentalists because it would mean extinction for a type of spotted owl. Controversies over endangered species will continue to become locally important issues.

Specific problems, such as radon exposure in private residences and asbestos exposure, especially in schools and public buildings, were discussed only briefly. Each of these areas of environmental policy has seen federal and state governments taking a variety of actions, and each has been involved in some degree of controversy (Cohen, 1986, p. 13; Krimsky & Plough, 1988, pp. 130-175; USEPA, 1984).

Another area of environmental controversy not discussed here is the development and use of genetically engineered organisms. The controversy over using the *ice minus bacterium,* a genetically manufactured microbe designed to protect agricultural crops from experiencing frost damage, may be a good case in point. Genetic engineers developed an organism that they felt had the capacity to potentially provide farmers and the general public with considerable cost savings from crop damage. These engineers felt they had plenty of reason to believe that the new microbe would be perfectly safe in the environment. Others were not so sure. Fearing the potential catastrophic effects on people if a new, genetically engineered, mutant organism had deleterious effects on people's health, many people sought to stop the testing of this microbe on strawberry crops in California (Krimsky & Plough, 1988, pp. 75-129). As genetic engineers develop new and more exotic materials, public policy will eventually have to either sanction or prevent the use of these materials, often without very much knowledge about the risks they might pose.

This book has not addressed issues of controversies surround potential and actual environmental damage from various nuclear and radioactive materials other than radon. Over the years, there has been considerable local concern over developing a reliance on nuclear-power generating facilities. Controversies surrounding locating such plants as the Diablo Canyon facility in California, the Seabrook nuclear plant in New Hampshire, and the Shoreham facility in New York will continue to be issues, especially if efforts to decrease America's reliance on foreign oil require a new, short-term push toward energy independence. Additionally, there will be increasing pressure to find a solution to disposing of the high- and low-level radioactive waste products from existing and functioning nuclear-power facilities. Spent nuclear rods, examples of high-level radioactive material, cannot continue to be stored on-site at each facility forever. Federal efforts to resolve this problem by prescribing the development of specific nuclear waste disposal sites are far from settled.

Although these issues were not discussed explicitly, the framework presented here may be fruitfully applied to help develop an independent understanding of them. Each of these controversies or issues possesses its own set of characteristics, and many of them are specific additional examples of the clashes of values discussed in Chapter 1. In varying ways, each also has its own policy history and policy-making process, and the policy-making process framework might well provide the foundation for sorting out the various events of this process.

References

Andrews, R. N. L. (1982). Cost-benefit analysis as regulatory reform. In D. Swartzman, R. A. Liroff, & K. G. Croke (Eds.), *Cost-benefit analysis and environmental regulations: Politics, ethics, and methods* (pp. 107-135). Washington, DC: The Conservation Foundation.

Andrews, R. N. L. (1988). Hazardous waste facility siting: State approaches. In C. E. Davis & J. P. Lester (Eds.), *Dimensions of hazardous waste politics and policy* (pp. 117-128). Westport, CT: Greenwood.

Arcury, T. A., Scollay, S. J., & Johnson, T. P. (1987). Sex differences in environmental concern and knowledge: The case of acid rain. *Sex Roles, 16*(9/10), 463-472.

Baldwin, M. F. (1987). Wetlands: Fortifying federal and regional cooperation. *Environment, 29*(7), 16-43.

Baram, M. S. (1980). Cost-benefit analysis: An inadequate basis for health, safety, and environmental regulatory decision making. In *Ecology Law Review, 9,* 473-531.

Barke, R. (1988). Hazardous wastes and the politics of policy change. In C. E. Davis & J. P. Lester (Eds.), *Dimensions of hazardous waste politics and policy* (pp. 147-162). Westport, CT: Greenwood.

Bellah, R. N., Madsen, R., Sullivan, W., Swidler, A., & Tipton, S. M. (1985). *Habits of the heart: Individualism and commitment in American society.* Berkeley: University of California Press.

Bernard, H. (1980). *The greenhouse effect.* New York: Harper Colophon.

Berry, M. A. (1984). *A method for examining policy implementation: A study of decision making for the national ambient air quality standards, 1964-1984.* Washington, DC: U.S. Environmental Protection Agency.

Biniek, J. P. (1986). Benefit-cost analysis: An evaluation. In S. Kamieniecki, R. O'Brien, & M. Clarke (Eds.), *Controversies in environmental policy* (pp. 136-152). Albany: State University of New York Press.

Blocker, T. J., & Eckberg, D. L. (1989). Environmental issues as women's issues: General concerns and local hazards. *Social Science Quarterly, 70*(3), 586-593.

Bosso, C. J. (1987). *Pesticides and politics: The life cycle of a public issue.* Pittsburgh: University of Pittsburgh Press.

Bowman, A. O'M. (1984). Intergovernmental and intersectoral tensions in environmental policy implementation: The case of hazardous waste. *Policy Studies Review, 4*(2), 230-244.

Bowman, A. O'M. (1988). Superfund implementation: Five years and how many cleanups? In C. E. Davis & J. P. Lester (Eds.), *Dimensions of hazardous waste politics and policy* (pp. 129-146). Westport, CT: Greenwood.

Brodeur, P. (1985). *Outrageous misconduct: The asbestos industry on trial.* New York: Pantheon.

Brody, C. J. (1984, September). Differences by sex in support for nuclear power. *Social Forces, 63*(1), 209-221.

Brown, W. M. (1984, May 28). Maybe acid rain isn't the villain. *Fortune,* pp. 170-174.

Bryner, G. C. (1987). *Bureaucratic discretion: Law and policy in federal regulatory agencies.* New York: Pergamon.

Buttel, F. H., & Flinn, W. L. (1976, September). Economic growth vs. the environment: Survey evidence. *Social Science Quarterly, 57*(2), 410-420.

Buttel, F. H., & Flinn, W. L. (1977, Winter). Conceptions of rural life and environmental concern. *Rural Sociology, 42*(4), 544-555.

Buttel, F. H., & Flinn, W. L. (1978a). The politics of environmental concern: The impacts of party identification and political ideology on environmental attitudes. *Environment and Behavior, 10,* 17-36.

Buttel, F. H., & Flinn, W. L. (1978b). Social class and mass environmental beliefs: A reconsideration. *Environment and Behavior, 10*(September), 433-450.

Caldwell, T. W., & Roos, L. L., Jr. (1971). Voluntary compliance and pollution abatement. In L. L. Roos, Jr. (Ed.), *The politics of ecosuicide* (pp. 236-267). New York: Holt, Rinehart & Winston.

Carson, R. (1962). *Silent spring.* Boston: Houghton Mifflin.

Catton, W. R., & Dunlap, R. E. (1978). Environmental sociology: A paradigm. *The American Sociologist, 13,* 41-49.

Clarke, L. (1989). *Acceptable risk? Making decisions in a toxic environment.* Berkeley: University of California Press.

Cohen, B. (1986, April). Radon: Our worst radiation hazard. *Consumer's Research,* p. 13.

Cohen, S. (1984). Defusing the toxic time bomb: Federal hazardous waste programs. In N. J. Vig & M. E. Kraft (Eds.), *Environmental policy in the 1980s: Reagan's new agenda* (pp. 273-291). Washington, DC: Congressional Quarterly Press.

Cohn, J. P. (1987). Chlorofluorocarbons and the ozone layer. *BioScience, 37*(9), 647-650.

Congressional Digest, Inc. (1985, December). The clean water controversy. *The Congressional Digest, 64*(12), 290-314.

Congressional Quarterly, Inc. (CQWR). (1981, December 19). Congress clears sewer grant legislation. *Congressional Quarterly Weekly Report, 39*(51), 2527-2529.

Congressional Quarterly, Inc. (CQWR). (1986, May 17). House passes safe drinking water legislation. *Congressional Quarterly Weekly Report, 44*(20), 1126-1127.

Cotgrove, S. F. (1982). *Catastrophe or cornucopia: The environment, politics, and the future.* New York: John Wiley.

Council on Environmental Quality. (1981). *Environmental quality.* Washington, DC: Government Printing Office.

Crotty, P. M. (1987, Spring). The new federalism game: Primacy implementation of environmental policy. *Publius: The Journal of Federalism, 17,* 53-67.

Davies, J. C., & Davies, B. S. (1975). *The politics of pollution* (2nd ed.). Indianapolis, IN: Pegasus.

Davis, C. E., & Lester, J. P. (Eds.). (1988). *Dimensions of hazardous waste politics and policy.* Westport, CT: Greenwood.

DeSanti, R. J. (1980). Cost-benefit analysis for standards regulating toxic substances under the occupational safety and health act: American Petroleum Institute v. OSHA. *Boston University Law Review, 60,* 115-143.

Dietz, T. M., & Rycroft, R. W. (1987). *The risk professionals.* New York: Russell Sage.

Doninger, D. (1978). Federal regulation of vinyl chloride: A short course in the law and policy of toxic substances control. In *Ecology Law Quarterly, 7* 497-677.

Downs, A. (1972). Up and down with ecology: The "issue-attention cycle." *The Public Interest, 2,* 38-50.

Dryzek, J. S. (1987). *Rational ecology: Environment and political economy.* New York: Basil Blackwell.

Dunlap, R. E., & Catton, W. R. (1979). Environmental sociology. *Annual Review of Sociology, 5,* 243-273.

Durant, R. (1984, July/August). EPA, TVA and pollution control: Implications for a theory of regulatory policy implementation. *Public Administration Review, 44*(4), 305-315.

Fiorino, D. J. (1990, January/February). Can problems shape priorities? The case of risk-based environmental planning. *Public Administration Review, 50*(1), 82-90.

Foegen, J. H. (1986). Contaminated water: The trickle down problem that's welling up fast. *The Futurist, 20*(2), 22-24.

Fortuna, R. C., & Lennett, D. J. (1987). *Hazardous waste regulation: The new era—an analysis and guide to RCRA and the 1984 amendments.* New York: McGraw-Hill.

Francis, R. S. (1983). Attitudes toward industrial pollution, strategies for protecting the environment, and environmental-economic trade-offs. *Journal of Applied Social Psychology, 13,* 310-327.

Freeman, A. M. (1978). *Current issues in U.S. environmental policy.* Baltimore, MD: Johns Hopkins University Press.

Gaines, S. E. (1977). Decisionmaking procedures at the Environmental Protection Agency. *Iowa Law Review, 62,* 839-908.

George, D. L., & Southwell, P. L. (1986). Opinion on the Diablo Canyon nuclear power plant. *Social Science Quarterly, 67*(4), 722-735.

Gorham, E. (1982, October). What to do about acid rain? *Technology Review,* 58-63.

Graedel, T. E., & Crutzen, P. J. (1989, September). The changing atmosphere. *Scientific American,* p. 63.

Grunbaum, W. (1988). Judicial enforcement of hazardous waste liability law. In C. E. Davis & J. P. Lester (Eds.), *Dimensions of hazardous waste politics and policy* (pp. 163-176). Westport, CT: Greenwood.

Hadden, S. G. (Ed.). (1984). *Risk analysis, institutions, and public policy.* New York: Associated Faculty Press.

Hamilton, L. C. (1985a). Concern about toxic wastes: Three demographic predictors. *Sociological Perspectives, 28,* 463-486.

Hamilton, L. C. (1985b). Who cares about water pollution? Opinions in a small-town crisis. *Sociological Inquiry, 55,* 170-181.

Hawkins, K. (1984). *Environment and enforcement: Regulation and the social definition of pollution.* Oxford, UK: Clarendon.

House, P. W., & Shull, R. D. (1985). *Regulatory reform: Politics and the environment.* New York: University Press of America.

Howard, R., & Perley, M. (1980). *Acid rain: The North American forecast.* Toronto: Anansi Press.

Ingram, H., & Mann, D. E. (1984). Preserving the clean water act. In N. J. Vig & M. E. Kraft (Eds.), *Environmental policy in the 1980s* (pp. 251-272). Washington, DC: Congressional Quarterly Press.

Jessup, D. H. (1988). *Guide to state environmental programs.* Washington, DC: Bureau of National Affairs.

Johnson, A. H. (1986, May). Acid deposition: Trends, relationships, and effects. *Environment, 28,* 6-11, 34-38.

Jones, C. O. (1974, May). Speculative augmentation in federal air pollution policy-making. *Journal of Politics,* 438-464.

Jones, C. O. (1975). *Clean air: The policies and politics of pollution control.* Pittsburgh: University of Pittsburgh Press.

Jones, P., Wigley, T., & Wright, P. (1986). Global temperature variation between 1861 and 1964. *Nature, 322,* 430-434.

Kamlet, K. S. (1979). *Toxic substances programs in U.S. states and territories: How well do they work?* Washington, DC: National Wildlife Federation.

Ketchum-Colwill, J. (1986, September). Safe drinking water law toughened. *Environment, 28*(7), 5-43.

Kraft, M., & Vig, N. (Eds.). (1988). *Technology and politics.* Durham, NC: Duke University Press.

Krimsky, S., & Plough, A. (1988). *Environmental hazards: Communicating the risks as a social process.* Dover, MA: Auburn House.

Kunreuther, H., & Ley, E. V. (Eds.). (1982). *The risk analysis controversy: An institutional perspective.* Berlin: Springer.

Ladd, E. C. (1982, February/March). Clearing the air: Public opinion and public policy on the environment. *Public Opinion, 5,* 19.

Lake, L. (1983, Summer). The environmental mandate: Activists and the electorate. *Political Science Quarterly, 98,* 215-233.

Lave, L. (1988). The greenhouse effect: What government actions are needed? *Journal of Policy Analysis and Management, 7*(3), 460-470.

Leaf, D. A. (1990, May). Acid rain and the clean air act. *Chemical Engineering Progress, 86,* 25-29.

Leape, J. P. (1980). Quantitative risk assessment in regulation of environmental carcinogens. *Harvard Environmental Law Review, 4,* 86-116.

Ledbetter, J. L. (1984). The federal role in funding clean water. In H. C. Reeves (Ed.), *Funding clean water* (pp. 49-59). Lexington, MA: Lexington Books.

Lester, J. O., Franke, J. L., Bowman, A. O'M., & Kramer, K. W. (1983). A comparative perspective on state hazardous waste regulation. In J. P. Lester & C. E. Davis (Eds.), *The politics of hazardous waste management* (pp. 212-233). Durham, NC: Duke University Press.

Leventhal, H. (1974). Environmental decision making and the role of the courts. *University of Pennsylvania Law Review, 122,* 509-555.

Levine, A. G. (1982). *Love Canal: Science, politics, and people.* Lexington, MA: Lexington Books.

Lieber, H. (1975). *Federalism and clean waters: The 1972 water pollution control act.* Lexington, MA: Lexington Books.

Lieber, H. (1983). Federalism and hazardous waste policy. In J. P. Lester & A. O'M. Bowman (Eds.), *The politics of hazardous waste management* (pp. 60-72). Durham, NC: Duke University Press.

Lindblom, C. (1980). *The policy making process.* Englewood Cliffs, NJ: Prentice-Hall.

Liroff, R. A. (1976). *A national policy for the environment: NEPA and its aftermath.* Bloomington: Indiana University Press.

Liroff, R. A. (1986). *Reforming air pollution regulation: The toil and trouble of EPA's bubble.* Washington, DC: The Conservation Foundation.

MacAvoy, P. W. (1979). *The regulated industries and the economy.* New York: Norton.

MacDonald, G. J. (1988). Scientific basis for the greenhouse effect. *Journal of Policy Analysis and Management, 7*(3), 425-444.

Mazmanian, D. A., & Nienaber, J. (1979). *Can organizations change?* Washington, DC: Brookings Institution.

Mazmanian, D. A., & Sabatier, P. A. (1983). *Implementation and public policy.* Glenview, IL: Scott, Foresman.

McStay, J. R., & Dunlap, R. E. (1983). Male-female differences in concern for environmental quality. *International Journal of Women's Studies, 6*(4), 291-301.

Meier, K. J. (1985). *Regulations: Politics, bureaucracy, and economics.* New York: St. Martin's Press.

Melnick, R. S. (1983). *Regulation and the courts: The case of the clean air act.* Washington, DC: Brookings Institution.

Milbrath, L. (1984). *Environmentalists: Vanguard for a new society.* Albany: State University of New York Press.

Mintzer, I. (1988). Living in a warmer world: Challenges for policy analysis and management. *Journal of Policy Analysis and Management, 7*(3), 445-459.

Mitchell, R. C. (1980). *Public opinion on environmental issues: Results of a national opinion survey.* Washington, DC: Council on Environmental Quality.

Mitchell, R. C. (1984). Public opinion and environmental politics in the 1970s and 1980s. In N. J. Vig & M. E. Kraft (Eds.), *Environmental policy in the 1980s: Reagan's new agenda* (pp. 51-74). Washington, DC: Congressional Quarterly Press.

Mohai, P. (1985, December). Public concern and elite involvement in environmental-conservation issues. *Social Science Quarterly, 66*(4), 820-838.

Molina, M. J., & Rowland, F. S. (1974). Stratospheric sink for chlorofluoromethanes: Chlorine atom catalyzed destruction of ozone. *Nature, 249,* 810-812.

Morell, D., & Magorian, C. (1982). *Siting hazardous waste facilities: Local opposition and the myth of preemption.* Cambridge, MA: Ballinger.

Morone, J. G., & Woodhouse, E. J. (1986). *Averting catastrophe: Strategies for regulating risky technologies*. Berkeley: University of California Press.

Mosher, L. (1982, June 12). Environmentalists, industry left cold by EPA bid for new pretreatment rules. *National Journal,* 1060.

National Academy of Sciences. (1977). *Decision making in the Environmental Protection Agency.* Washington, DC: Author.

National Academy of Sciences. (1983). *Changing climate.* Washington, DC: Author.

National Acid Precipitation Assessment Program (NAPAP). (1990, September). *Background on acidic deposition and the national acid precipitation assessment program* and *Assessment highlights.* Washington, DC: Author.

National Council on Air Quality. (1981). *To breathe clean air.* Washington, DC: Government Printing Office.

National Research Council (NRC). (1983). *Risk assessment in the federal government: Managing the process.* Washington, DC: National Academy Press.

National Research Council (NRC). (1986a). *Acid deposition: Long term trends.* Washington, DC: National Academy Press.

National Research Council (NRC). (1986b). *Ground water quality protection: State and local strategies.* Washington, DC: National Academy Press.

Nealy, S. M., Melber, B. D., & Rankin, W. L. (1983). *Public opinion and nuclear energy.* Lexington, MA: Lexington Books.

O'Brien, R. M., Clarke, M., & Kamieniecki, S. (1984, July/August). Open and closed systems of decision making: The case of toxic waste management. *Public Administration Review, 44*(4), 334-340.

O'Hare, M. (1984). Governments and source reduction of hazardous waste. *Hazardous Waste and Hazardous Material, 1*(3), 443-451.

Ophuls, W. (1977). *Ecology and the politics of scarcity.* San Francisco: Freeman.

Palumbo, D., & Maynard-Moody, S. (1991). *Contemporary public administration.* New York: Longman.

Passino, E. M., & Lounsbury, J. W. (1976). Sex differences in opposition to and support for construction of a proposed nuclear power plant. In P. Suedefelf & J. A. Russell (Eds.), *The behavioral basis of design* (Bk. 1, selected papers). New York: Van Nostrand Reinhold.

Pederson, W., Jr. (1981). Why the clean air act works badly. *University of Pennsylvania Law Review, 129,* 1059-1091.

Peskin, H. M., & Seskin, E. P. (Eds.) (1975). *Cost benefit analysis and water pollution policy.* Washington, DC: Urban Institute Press.

Platt, R. H. (1987, November). Coastal wetland management: The advance delegation approach. *Environment, 29*(9), 16-20, 38-43.

Portney, K. E. (1991a). *Siting hazardous waste treatment facilities: The NIMBY syndrome.* Dover, MA: Auburn House.

Portney, K. E. (1991b). Citizen roles in public environmental decision making. In R. A. Chechile (Ed.), *Environmental decision making.* New York: Van Nostrand Reinhold.

Portney, P. R. (Ed.). (1984). *Natural resources and the environment: The Reagan approach.* Washington, DC: Urban Institute Press.

Postel, S. (1986, March/April). Water for the future: On tap or down the drain? *The Futurist, 20* (2), 17-21.

Rahn, K. A., & Lowenthal, D. H. (1986, July). The acid rain whodunit. *Natural History, 95*(7), 62-65.

Raynor, S. (1984). Disagreeing about risk: The institutional cultures of risk management and planning for future generations. In S. Hadden (Ed.), *Risk analysis, institutions, and public policy*. New York: Associated Faculty Press.

Regens, J. L., Dietz, T. M., & Rycroft, R. W. (1983, March/April). Risk assessment in the policy-making process: Environmental health and safety protection. *Public Administration Review, 43*(2), 137-145.

Regens, J. L., & Rycroft, R. W. (1988). *The acid rain controversy*. Pittsburgh, PA: University of Pittsburgh Press.

Revkin, A. C. (1988, October). Endless summer: Living with the greenhouse effect. *Discover*, pp. 50-61.

Ripley, R. B., & Franklin, G. A. (1980). *Congress, the bureaucracy and public policy* (2nd ed.). Homewood, IL: Dorsey.

Ripley, R. B., & Franklin, G. A. (1982). *Bureaucracy and policy implementation*. Homewood, IL: Dorsey.

Robins, J., Landrigan, P., Robins, F., & Fine, L. (1985, September). Decision-making under uncertainty in the setting of environmental health regulations. *Journal of Public Health Policy, 6*(3), 333-362.

Rodgers, W. H., Jr. (1981). Judicial review of risk assessments: The role of decision theory in unscrambling the benzene decision. *Environmental Law, 11*, 301-320.

Rohr, J. (1988). Bureaucratic morality in the United States. *International Political Science Review, 9*, 167-179.

Roos, L. L., Jr., & Bohner, H. J. (1973). Compliance, pollution, and evaluation. In J. A. Caporaso & L. L. Roos, Jr. (Eds.), *Quasi-experimental approaches: Testing theory and evaluating policy* (pp. 271-280). Evanston, IL: Northwestern University Press.

Rosenbaum, W. A. (1977). *The politics of environmental concern* (2nd ed.). New York: Holt, Rinehart & Winston.

Rosenbaum, W. A. (1985). *Environmental politics and policy*. Washington, DC: Congressional Quarterly Press.

Russell, C. S., Harrington, W., & Vaughn, W. J. (1986). *Enforcing pollution control laws*. Washington, DC: Resources for the Future.

Schmandt, J. (1985, March/April). Managing comprehensive rule making: EPA's plan for integrated environmental management. *Public Administration Review, 45*(2), 309-318.

Schneider, K. (1990, October 28). Ambitious air pollution bill sent to White House. *The New York Times*, p. L28.

Schneider, S. H. (1989). *Global warming: Are we entering the greenhouse century?* San Francisco: Sierra Club Books.

Schneider, W. (1983, March 26). The environment: The public wants more protection, not less. *National Journal*, 676-677.

Schultz, G. (1974). *Ice age lost*. New York: Anchor Press/Doubleday.

Seidman, H., & Gilmour, R. (1986). *Politics, position, and power: From the positive to the regulatory state* (4th ed.). New York: Oxford University Press.

Shea, C. P. (1988). *Protecting life on earth: Steps to save the ozone layer* (Paper #87). Washington, DC: Worldwatch Institute.

Smith, R. A., Alexander, R. B., & Wolman, M. G. (1987, March 27). Water quality trends in the nation's rivers. *Science, 235*, 1607-1616.

Smith, V. K. (Ed.). (1984). *Environmental policy under Reagan's executive order*. Chapel Hill: University of North Carolina Press.

Snow, C. P. (1960). *The two cultures and the scientific revolution*. New York: Cambridge University Press.

Snow, C. P. (1964). *The two cultures: And a second look*. New York: Cambridge University Press.

Stewart, R. (1977). The development of administrative and quasi-constitutional law in judicial review of environmental decisionmaking—lessons from the clean air act. *Iowa Law Review, 62,* 713-769.

Swartzman, D., Liroff, R. A., & Croke, K. G. (Eds.). (1982). *Cost-benefit analysis and environmental regulations: Politics, ethics, and methods*. Washington, DC: The Conservation Foundation.

Tobin, R. J. (1984). Revising the clean air act: Legislative failure and administrative success. In N. Vig and M. Kraft (Eds.), *Environmental policy in the 1980s: Reagan's new agenda* (pp. 227-249). Washington, DC: Congressional Quarterly Press.

Tocqueville, A. de (1964). *Democracy in America*. New York: G. Dearborn. (Original work published 1838).

Tolley, G. S., Graves, P. E., & Blomquist, G. C. (1981). *Environmental policy: Elements of environmental policy (Vol. I)*. Cambridge, MA: Ballinger.

U.S. Council on Environmental Quality. (1975). *Environmental quality, 1975*. Washington, DC: Government Printing Office.

U.S. Environmental Protection Agency (USEPA). (1983, October). *Can we delay greenhouse warming?* Washington, DC: Author.

U.S. Environmental Protection Agency (USEPA). (1984, October). *Evaluation of the asbestos-in-schools identification and notification rule*. Washington, DC: Author.

U.S. Environmental Protection Agency (USEPA). (1990, September). *Reducing risk: Setting priorities and strategies for environmental protection*. Washington, DC: U.S. Environmental Protection Agency, Science Advisory Board, Relative Risk Reduction Strategies Committee.

U.S. General Accounting Office (GAO). (1980, November 14). *Costly wastewater treatment plants fail to perform as expected* (Report CED-81-9).

Van Liere, K. E., & Dunlap, R. E. (1980). The social bases for environmental concern. *Public Opinion Quarterly, 44,* 181-197.

Vig, N. J., & Kraft, M. E. (Eds.). (1988). *Environmental policy in the 1980s*. Washington, DC: Congressional Quarterly Press.

Wagner, K. D. (1988, March 10-12). *The evolving federal role in environmental policymaking and the development of waterbody management programs*. Paper presented at the annual meetings of the Western Political Science Association, San Francisco.

Whitaker, J. L. (1976). *Striking a balance: Environment and natural resources policy in the Nixon-Ford years*. Washington, DC: American Enterprise Institute.

White, L. (1982, September). U.S. mobile source emission regulations: The problems of implementation. *Policy Studies Journal, 11,*(1), 77-87.

White, L., Jr. (1967). The historical roots of our ecological crisis. *Science, 155,* 1203-1207.

Wilson, R., & Crouch, E.A.C. (1987). Risk assessment and comparisons: An introduction. *Science, 236,* 267-270.

Wynne, B. (1982). Institutional mythologies and dual societies in the management of risk. In H. Kunreuther & E. V. Ley (Eds.), *The risk analysis controversy: An institutional perspective* (pp. 127-143). Berlin: Springer.

Yeager, P. C. (1987, October). Structural bias in regulatory law enforcement: The case of the U.S. Environmental Protection Agency. *Social Problems, 34*(4), 330-344.

Zeckhauser, R. (1975, Fall). Procedures for valuing lives. *Public Policy, 23*(4), 419-464.
Zile, Z. L. (1974). Political history of the coastal zone management act. *Coastal Zone Management Journal, 1*(3), 235-274.
Zimmerman, R. (1988). Federal-state hazardous waste management policy implementation in the context of risk uncertainties. In C. E. Davis & J. P. Lester (Eds.), *Dimensions of hazardous waste politics and policy.* (pp. 177-201). Westport, CT: Greenwood.

Index

About the Author

Kent E. Portney is an Associate Professor of Political Science at Tufts University. He is the author of *Siting Hazardous Waste Treatment Facilities: The NIMBY Syndrome* and many articles about the environment, hazardous waste policy, and public risk perceptions toward the environment. He has also written extensively about public policy analysis and about citizen participation in American politics. He received his Ph.D. in Political Science from Florida State University in 1979.